My Mighty Son

A true story of endurance and
overcoming against the odds

Virág Wheeler-Mezei

Onwards and Upwards Publishers

3 Radfords Turf
Exeter
EX5 7DX

www.onwardsandupwards.org

Typeface: Sabon LT

Printed in the UK.

Graphic design:	LM Graphic Design
Illustrations:	Finola Stack
Cover photograph:	Barbara Leatham Photography
Other photographs:	Captured Magic Photography

ISBN 978-1-911086-54-3

Endorsement

I don't understand why really tough things happen to good people. Instead of turning their back on God, Virág and James turn towards Him with their questions, doubts, disappointments and frustrations and in doing so experience His peace in a remarkable way. Virág writes with passion and honesty and her beautiful heart as a mother shines throughout. Something special happens when we share our common humanity and fragility in the way Virág has done in this book.

Patrick Regan OBE
Founder and CEO of XLP

Author's Note

The story is absolutely true.

Some names have been changed to protect identities, but I have sought permission to include people's real names when possible. Every person mentioned in this book has helped me on my journey, and for this I thank each and every one.

Acknowledgements

Thank you to my family and true friends for being in my life; everyone from All Saints Weston, people in the UK, in Hungary and other countries who support and pray for us; it means a lot.

Thank you to everyone at Mack for opening my eyes and broadening my perspective.

Thank you to Patrick, who helped to birth the vision for this book and for willingly writing the foreword. Thank you to Gez, who helped with the proofreading.

Thank you to Eszter and Balint for your ongoing friendship.

Thank you to my lovely home group and the Oasis mums for supporting me in many ways, and to Jo for being there for me.

Thank you to my beloved grandma, who showed me how to start to communicate with God.

Thank you to my husband James for your support, your kindness, for your patience and your love, but above all for being an amazing daddy to Luke.

Thank you to Luke Jeffery and his team for their work in the editing and publishing process; for turning this into a reality.

Thank you to Finola Stack for the lovely illustrations throughout the book.

Thank you to Barbara Leatham Photography (cover) and Captured Magic Photography (rear cover and inside) for their wonderful photographs used in this book.

In loving memory of my grandma,
Mezei Mama.

A Letter to our Dearest Son

My Dear Luke,

I don't know if you will ever get to read this, but I tell you this same story every day when we are praying together at night time.

You had to be born here into our little lives for me (Mummy) to understand many things. We wanted you so much, and Daddy and I were overjoyed when you were born. I knew before you were born that you were a boy and started to call you Luki[1]. I felt like someone said this name constantly around my head and I just repeated it continuously; so you became Luke.

Your first months as a baby were lovely – we always made sure that you enjoyed fun, happy times with us.

But after five months a terrible illness came which you not only survived but, amazingly, you lived with. Even after many operations and stays in hospital you were still shining and showed us how to cope with it all. We tried to live a normal family life as far as possible. I'm sorry that there were so many hospital appointments; I know you didn't like them. And we tried to have as much time as we could at home rather than hospital. As you grew you were more aware of what was going on physically. You didn't like the nurses taking blood or the doctors examining your tummy and chest. It's understandable.

I am so proud of you because you taught me to be positive, not to worry and to be happy for others – and about love. You are able to offer much love to everyone, to each as an individual. Most importantly, you showed me how not to be afraid or scared about death, and I again realised that God is here with us, looking after us and that he never lets us down. Luki, you are a light in our lives. You are a really unique and special boy and we love you so much. Thank you for everything. You will always shine in our lives.

Anya (Mummy) and Ada (Daddy)

---

[1] Pronounced Lukey

My Mighty Son

Contents

My Mighty Son

FOREWORD

This is the story of a journey that few of us have to take; it is only for the bravest. Virág and James are two young people who are talented, bright and attractive. James, as you might expect, is English, Virág is Hungarian. They met in Wales. Soon after their beautiful marriage and reception in a castle in Hungary, they came to live in one of the loveliest cities in England: Bath. There were few, if any, clouds in the sky. Virág worked with children, James in financial services. After a while Virág became pregnant; no one could have been more delighted and thrilled than both of them. Luki – or Luke – was born.

Luke seemed a very healthy baby. They made (and still do) a lovely family. And then their lives changed suddenly and drastically. Luke became unwell at around six months old. He was admitted to the local hospital and then was transferred to Bristol for radical emergency brain surgery for an aggressive brain tumour.

Subsequently, he had treatment upon treatment, hospital visit upon hospital visit, surgery, chemotherapy and pioneering radiotherapy. Luke has seen more of the inside of hospitals and of hospital theatres (for surgery) than almost all who will read his story. He is now three.

But this is a story of triumph in the midst of pain, frustration, bewilderment and uncertainty; of peace and confidence where normally there would be none. To have a seriously sick child is a test that most of us cannot begin to appreciate. It is a test of emotions that soar to the hope of healing, only to be crashed by further bad news. It is a test of our trust in those who have the life of a precious child frequently in their hands. It is a test of marriage, and principally of two devoted parents who seek to give constant care to their beloved son and who now must live out vows, made in a few seconds on a beautiful day, in the cauldron of stress and uncertainty. But above all for Virág and James, it was a test of their faith in a God who cares and who has everything in his hands.

Few precious things are achieved without struggle. But through the great and continuing struggle for James, Virág and Luke, beautiful things have come to birth. Out of the myriad questions about God, faith, healing and heaven has come a new confidence that whatever happens in the future, Luke will never be outside God's care and presence.

Virág and James' families and friends have provided unceasing care and support. Beautiful and unforgettable moments have been shared on the beach, in parks, at birthday parties, on an epic train journey from Bath to Budapest, in Hungary and England. But at the centre of it all is Luke himself – brave, prayerful, aware of God's presence, putting his lips together to say amen, putting his hands together spontaneously to pray, strong and sensitive, lapping up all the love that is around him. It was the Prophet Isaiah who said, "...and a little child shall lead them."[2] Truly through such a storm of cancer, pain and treatment, he has led his family and scores of others into a deeper appreciation of life and God's love. It's a hard way to learn this, but it is also an invitation to all who read to discover for themselves that with God nothing is ever lost and, above all, that he wants to be Emmanuel, God with us – if only we would let him.

Rev. Patrick Whitworth

---

[2] Isaiah 11:6

INTRODUCTION

Trusting in the Lord

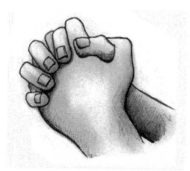

I waited patiently for the Lord to help me, and he turned to me and heard my cry. He lifted me out of the pit of despair, out of the mud and the mire. He set my feet on solid ground and steadied me as I walked along. He has given me a new song to sing, a hymn of praise to our God. Many will see what he has done and be amazed. They will put their trust in the LORD.

Psalm 40:1-3

This book is about my personal transformation – how I grew in faith and found a new friend who helped me through a difficult journey.

Faith? Your reaction might be, "I am not interested in a Christian book." You might not even believe in God. But I'm hoping that even if you aren't a Christian, you can find some useful words, thoughts and ideas to help in a situation you or someone close to you might be facing, perhaps even a serious illness with a family member. I want to let you know that you do not need to be afraid. God is with you – if you will just call for him. Everyone has their own story, and I would like to share mine with you.

Miracles do happen and you just need to open your eyes to really see them. My aim is not to change you – no-one changed me either – but it's never too late to trust in God. God is not just someone to turn to when the going gets tough; he is in your day-to-day life, whatever ups and downs you're going through. You just need to be able to see it.

You never think it will happen to you. I certainly didn't expect to face the challenges that I did. And I didn't expect to be writing a book about them by the age of thirty. But after a long church weekend away at Lee Abbey in Devon, I heard a voice telling me, "Write it down," and then I received encouragement from people that I really should go ahead and record everything that has happened.

So I have recorded events as they occurred, as accurately as possible, in the hope that this will benefit you or maybe someone you know. If you have a friend or family member whose story is similar, perhaps consider buying a copy for them too.

CHAPTER ONE

Growing Up in Hungary

All of them were filled with the Holy Spirit and began to speak in other tongues as the Spirit enabled them.

Acts 2:4

I am Hungarian but God has given me a special gift – of speaking and writing in English! How amazing, how funny that I should be writing a book in another language!

I am not from a Christian family and so I didn't know how to live as a Christian in my younger years, but someone important in my life opened my eyes. Even after that, it was a process. Everyone struggles with their faith. I did too. But often, struggling with faith doesn't just happen at one time in somebody's life. It can go on. This happened with me.

When I was little, my grandma, my dad's mum, moved in with us. She had her own room downstairs and I often saw her praying in her room. Actually, at first I didn't know quite what she was up to; she put her hands together, closed her eyes, and I used to sit down next to her quietly. I asked her what she was doing and why. She explained to me that she was praying to God to help her and give her strength.

I was so curious about this new thing I had discovered someone doing. I wanted to know what it was about, and who this God was who heard her prayers, and whether he answered back. So from then on I kept this 'God matter' in my mind, thinking about it from time to time. And I started to talk to God. I didn't know much about praying – how to pray, when to pray, what to pray – but I started to ask for things in my prayers: to get good marks in my schoolwork, or to have a good weekend with my family, or for God to give me a certain boy to be my boyfriend, for example. Really childish things.

I had many questions in my mind and started to go to the Catholic church in my village, where I had been baptised as a baby, listening to what was said. The priest offered Bible study after school for a few of us. It was really interesting and after some time I went on to have my First Communion, aged twelve. I also learned a bit about Christian traditions such as Easter, Christmas and Pentecost.

We had another church in the village, a Reformed (Protestant) church, where some of my old friends used to go, and they had many children's and evening activities. This was in contrast to the Catholic church which didn't have any such things going on. One day my friends who went to the Reformed church were practising for their Confirmations. I wanted to know how that was different from ours at the Catholic church. I liked the way that during the Communion part of the service at the Reformed church they had bread instead of a wafer, and how they used the words and sang worship songs differently. So this created a struggle within me.

Then I had my first experience of God's Holy Spirit. I had been questioning myself and God: is it alright that I'm going to that church as well as the Catholic church? A warm feeling came over me and I heard a voice which comforted me with the words, "You belong to me wherever you go." This was strange and scary at the same time. Of course I had no idea what was happening. Who was affecting my feelings? Who said that? But I listened to my heart and went to both the churches in my village, and I enjoyed listening to the Bible stories.

In the Catholic church I helped out with preparing Communion, reading short passages from the Bible, collecting the monetary offerings from the congregation and sometimes counting the money too. And in the other church, the Reformed church, I sang in the choir and acted in the nativity at Christmas time and played the piano. For me it was more about having fun than about learning and understanding Jesus Christ.

When I was thirteen, my beloved grandma passed away and I missed her very much, as I still do. We had been very close. Because of her illness, she couldn't hear very well. I was the only person who cared to relay to her what other people were asking from her when they wanted to talk to her. She could lip-read my words and that was just enough for her.

Over the years that she lived with us, we had lots of great conversations, and one of the more memorable ones took place when I was aged twelve. She told me all about growing up and that the first signs of becoming a mature woman are this and that... From then on, she always talked about it and helped me to be prepared. She even asked me if she could be the first person I told when the signs came, to which I happily agreed. On the very same day that we received a phone call from the hospital informing us that she had passed away, I got my first period. I found myself simultaneously crying and smiling, as I couldn't tell her what had happened to me, but then I had a sense that she knew anyway wherever she was in heaven. The first person I told straightaway was my dad. How funny, because I could have told my mum first, but I was a Daddy's girl. Daughters often have a great love for their daddies. Now I know that my period starting was a sign from God, which made losing her easier to bear.

Grandma is still in my heart and I have a framed photograph in our bedroom of her holding me when I was a baby. Just to see her smile on the picture every day is encouraging and still helps me. But at that time I felt very upset and angry, asking, "Why did she need to die?" For a long time, I didn't receive any answers – and I stopped going to church for a while.

It was soon time for me to start secondary school, or rather the Hungarian equivalent – it's the second school that children attend, from fourteen to eighteen, so it starts a lot later than in the UK. This was a big step for me. Not only was it a new school but it was not in the village where I lived. Now I had to travel to the nearest town for schooling.

One day at secondary school, I thought I had a conversation with my grandma. I know it sounds strange but she answered back. I spoke to the priest from the Reformed church about this and he told me that I could not talk to her anymore because she had to go to heaven to be happy.

I replied, "But she was happy with us."

Then he explained that she would be even happier than before, because in heaven there is no illness or disease and she could see her other family members.

I stopped talking with my grandma but it was hard to understand what heaven was all about. So I didn't bother; I didn't care about 'God stuff'. Yet all through my teenage years, I had a voice in my head saying, "I will never fail you. I will never abandon you."[3] This Bible verse is still with me these days.

I never had Christian friends around me, and in fact the only Christians around me were my two grandmas; they truly believed but I never asked them or anyone else about God. I lived in a small village in Hungary and the church was mainly made up of very old people; but they never looked happy there, just solemn, serious and, as I recall, with somewhat sad faces. They were people who had lost their families or friends. Sometimes I saw babies being christened, and that made a nice change. But I thought, "Is that what church is about? A place to go and be sad and cry?" I didn't want to go to church and be sad because it's not what I expected out of life.

As I lived and progressed through secondary school, I had ups and downs, as everyone does. I had a really good friend called Niki who knew everything about me and my life, just as I did hers. We went to school together on the bus in the early mornings and came home or just spent time somewhere in town together. Sometimes we didn't go to our lessons but instead went to a cafe around the corner to chat. Despite seeing each other all the time we never could finish our conversations – there was always much more to talk about! Then we ended up going to different colleges. She was studying to become a

---

[3] Hebrews 13:5

paramedic and I went to another college to study Journalism and Cultural Management on a four-year course.

At college I knew God wanted to speak to me but I didn't want to listen. So I tried to forget about him, not to know or even think about him, and most importantly not to believe in him.

I loved history and talking about the media from the past and current times, and listened attentively to lectures. As often happens at this time in your life, I met lots of people. Many of my friends at the time, some of whom are still my friends, believed in *something*, but it was something *else* and not God. So I tried listening to both sides of the debate to consider different opinions about why the Earth exists, what the meaning of life is, how to explain miracles and healings, and so on. I read my daily horoscope and when I read something positive I was happy and looked forward to that thing happening to me. But the good thing I'd been promised didn't happen. I read very many books, and I even went to a Feng Shui session and used what I learned there to change the layout of our flat in different ways, for good health, to find a good job etc. But nothing *big* happened.

I had a job (a few, in fact, but not concurrently) as well as going to college. I lived in Tiszavasvari, the closest town to the village of Tiszadob where my family lived, with my boyfriend Peti. I think he really wanted me to be someone professional with a good job, and because I loved him, I did everything for him. We were together for five years but during the last two years of our relationship I felt under a great deal of pressure from him. He had a games console with a steering wheel, pedals and a special driving chair, and he would sit for hours and hours 'driving' without talking to me. I always tried to busy myself with my own interests – cards and craft, or studying. I loved and still enjoy making greetings cards. I don't like buying them because I prefer putting time, effort and feeling into making cards for people. So while Peti was at home 'driving', I would make cards or go to see my friends in the next door flat, or return home to my village to see my parents and go for a walk with our dog Bendi.

During our relationship, I also lived for a while in Budapest as an au pair and it was good to taste the big city life. My older brother Matyi lived there and we used to meet up from time to time and catch up on news. It sounds funny now but for a large part of my childhood I had talked in an imaginary foreign language; I thought that I could speak a very special different language that only I could understand. And I had always imagined living abroad later in life.

In 2006, when I was nineteen, I took the opportunity to go to Oxford to live with a Hungarian family to look after their child during the day, like an au-pair. This was with Peti's brother's family so I already knew them reasonably well. It was good to be far away from him and I had had enough of college because of the pressure from Peti, so I thought that moving to Oxford for a while would give me some space and time to myself. I didn't spend a long time in Oxford, just a few months, but it was good to be an adult and more independent. I really loved their little boy Gergo, who was nine months old when I started looking after him. I had always liked children and could talk in a baby language – different from my imaginary foreign language – with them. We had so much fun. We went to see the ducks in the park, went to baby clubs, read nursery rhymes at the library, that kind of thing.

His mother, Edina, sent me on an evening English course for beginners. That was the first time I really learned some basic English. Although we had been taught some English at secondary school, for whatever reason I had learned German instead and didn't care about English. I now made some friends with fellow English-learners and went out with them for meals a few times. The times together were very amusing; our English was so basic that we had to draw the things we wanted to say!

Then a few months later I moved back in with Peti. To be honest, it wasn't great; I wasn't happy at all. We had numerous arguments and my dad was sad to see me so unhappy. But my previous experiences were not to be forgotten; I had gained a great love for children.

After a while my dad offered, or rather requested, that I would move back home. I did this – Peti and I split up – and I got my old room back at my parents' house in my home village, Tiszadob. As you can imagine (or perhaps you have experienced it yourself), it was very strange to live with my parents again. And some people in the village came to the wrong conclusions.

One day, out of the blue, I had an epileptic fit. It was an unusual type of fit in which I was found laughing in my sleep. So I went to hospital for a week to have many tests, and there I met an elderly

Christian lady who prayed for me. To avoid stress and another fit, I gave up the job I had working in the local police station. And around the same time, I also gave up my college studies after four years. I had so many exams. Surprisingly, but happily, the epilepsy never reoccurred.

I had taken out a student loan, and I had to pay back the money somehow, even if it had all been for nothing in the end. So the next job I managed to get was in a clothes boutique. At work, I enjoyed folding the clothes, chatting with the customers and sometimes there was a bit of added drama when clothes were shoplifted. I was lucky because I still had some friends in the local police force who would come to check if everything was fine in the shop and with me. When the store got busy, I phoned someone else to come and help for a while.

One day, a boy whom I had known as a child, Tamas, came to see me at the boutique. It was quite a surprise; he didn't actually live in the village but happened to be visiting his grandparents who lived on our road. We had hardly spoken over the years, but we occasionally saw each other around the village. Now he asked me to go for a walk that evening to get to know me better. I agreed and we ending up talking a lot and carried on meeting in the evenings for a while. Then one day he told me he was in love with me.

I was a bit cautious about starting a new relationship straightaway after splitting up with Peti. Tamas had already had a very eventful life. He lost his dad when he was just a little boy and, moreover, he actually witnessed the death, which was due to an accident while they were swimming in a river. He had rather odd friends and didn't always have a job; he sometimes had too much to drink and told me that he took other things as well.

In spite of this we continued to chat and meet up after I'd finished work, and spent hours just talking. Sometimes I went to his grandparents' house, sometimes to his mum's house in Debrecen, and sometimes he came to ours. I knew his sister and his mum; they are lovely people. Since then we kept meeting and I tried to convince him it would be a good idea to get and hold on to a job, as he lived with his mum and the money would be useful to help with bills, or to pay for things himself instead of relying on his mother. Sometimes he called me really late at night, after having 'had a few' to drink, to tell me he loved me and never wanted to leave me. I tried to explain to him that whilst I enjoyed his company and sharing a good time with him, I wasn't ready to think about things that seriously but I enjoyed hanging out with him. I really appreciated that in some ways he changed himself for me; that was really nice. He became different with people, kinder and more helpful. He also got back in touch with, and went to see, his late father's parents whom he hadn't seen for a long time.

Eventually we lost touch. I can't remember exactly how but I think it was when we had an argument about his heavy drinking. I started chatting online with other people.

As you can see, God wasn't involved in my life at that time and I didn't really care about him. I wasn't under control. But I desperately wanted to know how the Earth had come to exist, and where had water, animals, plants, people and life come from? I knew *someone* must have made it all; there had to have been a Creator. By this time, I only occasionally went to the Catholic church with my maternal grandma, and this was mainly just to see her as she lived on a small, bumpy road on the far side of the village. I didn't listen to much of the service itself as the priest just mumbled and rushed through and I felt that he didn't really care about God himself either. He went through the motions but hardly talked with people after the meeting and kept looking at his watch as he needed to go to the next village to take a service there. As far as I remember, none of the Catholic priests lived in my village and they were responsible for churches in several of the surrounding villages and towns.

One day I was messaging a Hungarian guy, Pali, over the Internet, who told me he lived in the UK. We started chatting every single day and then he came home to Hungary to visit his family so we arranged to meet at his parents' house. You might think at this point that I had too many boys in my life. Perhaps so, but I was trying to find Mr Right. So we met up and Pali told me that he wanted me to go and live with him in the UK. I wanted to go too and I told my parents so. I wanted to try to make a success of something and didn't want to get stuck in the village. My parents were very surprised and, in fact, so was I; Pali and I had only just met and it was unlike me to act so spontaneously. But I wasn't happy at home and wanted to go to the UK again, having enjoyed my time in Oxford two years previously. It also made financial sense as my phone bills from calling to Pali had exceeded my wages; the cost of calling abroad was so high. I decided I would give it a go.

CHAPTER TWO

Moving to the UK

The Lord keeps watch over you as you come and go, both now and forever.

Psalm 121: 8

On June 3rd, 2008, my mum's birthday, I turned a big corner in my life when I moved to the UK, to Cardiff. Everyone always asks me, "Why did you come to Britain?" Well, I think a great answer is that *God wanted me to come.*

I lived with Pali in a typical large Victorian house with several other Hungarians, a Polish guy and a Welsh guy. In the beginning we had good times and he showed me around the city. He had a job as a factory worker and I wanted to learn English as well as find my own job because I knew some basic English from my time in Oxford. In many ways, it was hard to live with other Hungarians because it didn't help me to learn the English language and I was too shy to talk with the others.

One day we had a house party. I never really liked them because it would be loud. I went out to see if I could meet any people whom I didn't know. I got chatting with a Hungarian couple called Eszter and Balint; talking about which part of Hungary they came from, what they were doing in Cardiff and how long they've lived there, that kind of thing. Balint worked at the same factory as Pali and another of our housemates, which is how they'd come to be at the party. After a long chat it turned out that Eszter and I had arrived on the same flight! Looking back, I realised I recognised her face from the airport departure lounge; she had rushed back from the toilet to the desk as she had lost her wedding ring.

Eszter was disappointed that for all the time she'd lived in Cardiff – about a month by now – we hadn't known that both of us were just at home most of the time, whereas we could have met up. She waited all day for Balint to come home from work. She was too shy even to go out for a walk or to the shops as she couldn't speak any English. After the party, we met up every single day and became best friends!

One day, Pali and I were walking along Albany Road near where we lived and someone handed me a leaflet about an English course for beginners.

I rushed back home and called Eszter. "There is an opportunity to learn basic English!" I said. It was for international people who had never learned English before or who had come to the UK with poor English, like me. I desperately wanted to find a job because I didn't feel comfortable being at home all day. Even though I had a hundred English books around me, it wasn't a big help as no-one gave me lessons. Eszter was really happy about the course, although she also felt nervous about starting something new like this.

To start with, we needed to do written and spoken tests to assess our ability and decide where to put each of us. Because she didn't know any English and wanted me to be in the same class, I asked them to be with her. My English wasn't good but I knew a few words and I was happy that I could ask them.

I didn't realise at first that the course I was attending week after week was in a church building. For me, I only thought of churches as looking like the Hungarian pictures in my head, and this church building was nothing like those. To look back on my naiveté is really amusing! I discovered the truth when one day we went from the hall where the lessons took place to get something from the other room, and I saw in large letters high up on the wall, "Jesus Christ is Lord."

I said to myself, "Ah, here you are again. What do you want?"

The familiar answer came immediately: "I will never fail you. I will never abandon you."

One day I received an email from Tamas to say he had just lost his best friend in a motorbike accident; the friend had only recently bought the bike. Then he told me that he was so lost without me and wherever I was he would come to find me as he wanted to live with me. I felt rather angry with his former behaviour – not listening to what I was saying, and not answering his phone for days after an argument. So I said to him, "I am happy with my new life. Please don't make this harder. And I know you. I know that you will disappear again and not keep in touch for days."

I think he had a lot on his mind at that time and was confused. The next day I received an email from his sister Dora to say he had died. You can probably work out what had happened. I just couldn't believe it and I was so upset. I cried all day at work. Then, for the first time in a long time, I prayed, "Dear God, forgive me what I have done in the past. I haven't been looking for you but now I am in great pain and I am sure you know that. Please let him go to heaven and be with you. Help his family; give them strength." I was in pain and asked myself many questions, but mainly, did he do it because of me? My parents tried to talk me out of thinking this. I wasn't able to go to his funeral but my dad went for me and passed on a message from me to his sister and his mum. He is still in my heart and I light a candle in his memory on his birthday or whenever I feel like it.

Just around this time, Pali and I split up, and I can see the hand of God was leading me in this. The relationship just didn't work between us and I wanted to move out as soon as I could. I now had a job. One of the girls I was living with had given my CV to her manager, and I had got a job as a cleaner at a care home. So I moved out from the house with Pali and into a room where I found my happiness and peace. My new housemates, young women like me from all over Eastern Europe, were lovely. As the Bible says, "God is working in you, giving you the desire and the power to do what pleases him."[4] The funny thing about the house was that it was right opposite the church where I studied English. I couldn't believe how close I was. It seemed like God was drawing me to himself, that he wanted me to reach out to him again and be closer to him.

I asked someone from church who helped at the English lessons when the church services were. The first service I went to was amazing, and I found myself wondering, can this really be a church service? There was a live band with drums, electric guitars, piano and vocalists playing fantastic music. Although I hardly understood the worship songs and the service, I didn't mind being there. Somehow I knew that with time I would understand. But it felt unfamiliar and I asked myself, "Where is the priest? Why isn't the church leader wearing special clothes for the service? Why do they change the speaker every Sunday? Why do people raise their hands when they sing? What's that pool at the front with lots of water?" I didn't know much at that time about other types of churches and other Christian traditions.

Again I heard, "You belong to me wherever you go." I read a book which said, "No matter where you go in the world today, you can find some kind of church building to worship in." Then I realised that I was in the right place and I knew, I felt, that God had a plan for me and for my life.

In spite of my poor English, I tried to find out more and more about the church and the people there. I enjoyed going whenever I could and gradually learned more. I discovered that the church members were lovely, welcoming people who really cared for one another and prayed for others. I couldn't believe how different it was from the village in which I had grown up. They held an evening called 'International Café' once a week which provided the opportunity to get to know other international people in the area and people from church. They were all Christian people, with happy faces, providing a calm and relaxed atmosphere. I'm sure everyone had their own problems but they didn't show them as openly as in my village. As well as the hospitality provided at the International Cafe, every Sunday an elderly couple called Dennis and Freda invited people from

---

[4] Philippians 2:13

church for Sunday lunch, usually students and international people like me.

I was still far from God and I didn't pray much. Growing up, I didn't have a bible, but when I came to the UK my mum's mum gave hers to me as a gift, something from her to keep with me. This particular Hungarian Bible translation was really difficult to read, as it was written in quite old Hungarian, but I kept it and sometimes had a look in it. I said to myself that I would never be able to understand those words! Eventually I lost interest in trying to read it – but I still wanted to know about God, just in a different way.

If you wonder what faith really is, the Bible says, "Faith is the confidence that what we hope for will actually happen; it gives us assurance about things we cannot see."[5] It takes a lifetime to learn, and I knew there was still much to discover and understand. But how wonderful that I was interested in God and no other form of spirituality!

My friends Eszter and Balint used to come with me to church when we had days off from work on Sundays. A short while later, Eszter also got a job at the care home where I worked, and I was really blessed to have her as a friend. She was always by my side and I was there for her. We used to go out and about to discover Cardiff and the surrounding area. Eszter and Balint called me their "daughter" as they are half a generation older than me and without children of their own. I felt part of their family and had gained 'second parents'. It was good to know people from the church and to do activities with them.

I was now happy – settled in my new 'home', spending enjoyable time with Eszter and Balint, and meeting new people at the International Café.

---

[5] Hebrews 11:1

CHAPTER THREE

Meeting James

"For I know the plans I have for you," says the Lord. "They are plans for good and not for disaster, to give you a future and a hope."

Jeremiah 29:11

One rainy late winter Sunday when I went to the church service with Eszter and Balint the church was full and the three of us found some empty seats. There was an empty seat next to me but I knew someone was sitting there as there was a helmet and glass of water on the floor. Then a guy came in and I stood up to let him sit down on the empty seat next to me.

"Hi!" he greeted me.

"Hi!"

And then immediately the service started. From the corner of my eye I looked at him and found him attractive, and I think he liked me too.

After the service a friend called Max came to say hello and then, out of nowhere, suddenly the same guy came and stood next to him. Max introduced him to me as "James" – but that was all that happened. Then Dennis and Freda invited me to their home for lunch, as they often did. They gave me a lift, as they lived a few miles away, and we overtook Max and James cycling on the road – I didn't know they were also coming to lunch!

Usually for this shared Sunday meal the guests helped with the cooking, before we had a pre-meal tea, coffee, biscuit and a chat. On this occasion I helped with washing up some of the cooking utensils and pans used during the early stages of cooking and then James came next to me and started to cook something yellow. I asked him what it was. My English was still poor and I felt very nervous and uncomfortable that I couldn't have a proper conversation with someone whom I found attractive. That made it a bit difficult. But James was kind towards me.

A week later, on my day off, I was invited by Elaine from church to a day out at St Fagan's National History Museum. I invited Max as well because I knew him from International Cafe. We walked around the museum but I spent most of the time with Elaine because Max spent the whole time in the section about languages, reading the information; he was very interested in this topic. At the end, as I hadn't really had a chance to talk with him, I asked him if he would like to come around to chat or watch a film with me sometime, and he kindly agreed.

A few days later Max texted to ask if a friend could come too but he didn't say who.

"Great!" I replied. "I will cook dinner for us. Are you happy with Bolognese?"

Max said, "Anything you want. That's fine." However, after I had finished food shopping he texted me again to say that his friend was vegetarian, so I had to go back shopping to buy pizzas.

When Max and his friend arrived, I was very surprised that it was James who was with him, the guy whom I'd met in the church. Max told me they were housemates.

We watched a film whilst sitting side by side on the bed, as there wasn't much space in my room. It was a comedy – Evan Almighty – and we all laughed loudly. I brought the pizzas in during the film, including a vegetarian one for James. I also had a large box of chocolates and sweets that I always kept topped up in my room. The guys were either side of me and they laughed that I had so many. Then after the film we chatted about what everyone did for a living, with the help of the Internet to translate key words because of the limitations in our communication. Next to James on the bed he had laid out three mobile phones. He explained that one was for personal communications, one for business, and a third was for... It was a word I couldn't understand – something like 'saver' when translated from English to Hungarian and back again! We laughed so much trying to overcome the language barrier. I asked, "Are you going out on the street to save someone's life or something?" Later I came to understand what he did as he and Max used acting and drawings to communicate! It turned out he was a 'Search and Rescue' volunteer. I also found myself impressed when I discovered that James was in his final year at university studying Politics.

We had so much fun that night. A while after they had left, I received a text message from James who thanked me for the evening and said the food was nice. He promised to cook for me at his home next time. I found myself feeling something I had never felt before – a warm and happy feeling. As it turned out, he didn't end up cooking for me as he kept coming to my home to eat. We kept in touch using the vogue-but-aging MSN Messenger (instant messaging) and text messaging over the next few days.

On February 12th, 2009, on my brother Matyi's birthday, James visited my home and we spent a long time talking. We lay on the bed and just gazed at each other for hours and hours and, eventually, he kissed me. This was the kiss I had waited for, for so long – feeling in love with someone, feeling butterflies in my stomach. I couldn't believe it when James said he had never kissed anyone before. I felt so happy and excited.

James was going to be away for the weekend to participate in a walking competition. It already felt strange to be separated from him, as I felt I now belonged to him. But he did come to the evening church service on Sunday. Afterwards, we both went to another church where a friend of mine was playing music. There they were holding a Fairtrade quiz night starting with food and drink and with lots of young people. We were sitting in a circle on the floor and I looked across at James sitting on the other side. Finally, he came to sit next to me and we held each other's hands tightly, and he told me that he had missed me.

James and I hadn't been together a long time, a matter of weeks, when I had to return to Hungary for a fortnight to visit my family and friends and to celebrate my birthday at home. The tickets had already been booked before I had started seeing James, and it was now hard to leave him. Moreover, it was hard to tell him how sad I felt about all this because I couldn't speak much English. He took me to Bristol Airport and it was difficult saying our goodbyes. I felt pulled in two directions; I was happy to go home and see my family, but I felt insecure in our very early relationship. What if he would decide, "That's it!" and leave me?

We tried to keep in touch while I was away using the Internet and he phoned me on my birthday, wishing me "boldog szulinapot"[6]. The memory of this moment is particularly vivid because I was on a little ferry crossing a river with my dad and it was rather noisy.

The two weeks flew by quickly and soon I was back in his arms at the airport. While I had been away, James had looked after my 'mouse' and laptop. My mouse is my favourite soft toy that I've had since I was a newborn baby; it was very important to me so I asked him to look after it. It's a large mouse, the size of a teddy bear, and James showed me photos of my mouse doing things during my absence: using the laptop, drinking from a bottle of water, and reading a "Learn Welsh" book.

Soon it was spring and Eastertime, and James took me to Devon to introduce me to his mum. James had grown up in Devon; his parents had divorced when he was five years old, and he and his mum moved from the Midlands to Devon a few years after this. I was so nervous because of my English and worried about how I would be able to understand his mum and whether she would be able to understand me. She has a strong Christian faith and James has too, which was a bit difficult for me as God was still far from me at this time. I slept in a different room from James which felt very odd; we knew that nothing was going to 'happen', same room or not.

---

[6] "Happy birthday!" in Hungarian

When James came to my home in the evenings, he used to stay until really late, usually around two o'clock in the morning, but then went home. I found it really strange to have to sleep without him. We talked a lot about Christianity and I was always afraid that I wasn't good enough in his mum's eyes because I wasn't a 'real' Christian. Also at times we had differences of opinion which were difficult to work through. For example, in a relationship I felt it was important to live together, as that's how you get to know one another. Often I had to learn to understand and accept that James had different ideas, a different background. I had so much love for him and because of this I could live with these differences.

There were also difficult days when I just wanted to 'be physical' with James. He had told me I was his first girlfriend which led me to some silly concerns: "Is it worth being with him when he has applied Christian principles all his life?" But I loved being with him very much and we hugged and kissed a lot. We had a talk about his Christian values such as saving God's gift of sex until marriage and I was surprised by this viewpoint. It felt like a challenge and I was interested to see how long I could cope with it. James is a really good man and he is very caring. It seems that God wanted us together and we continued to enjoy the time in each other's company, whilst I tried not to think about the lack of sex and focussed on getting to know his heart and personality.

Over the coming months, I got to know James' dad, who came to visit him every month or so and went walking with him, and also James' brother and sister, nine and eleven years older than him respectively. They were all nice people and I was so worried whether they would accept me into their lives because of my weak English and being a foreigner. I was shy and didn't talk much. But they always made encouraging comments about my English and how it was developing, so over time I felt much better.

James and I often went for walks on a hill near Caerphilly – a place we called 'Caerphilly Mountain'. He had rented a warehouse in Caerphilly for his business, which I enjoyed visiting. He had set the business up a few years ago selling Fairtrade products like coffee, tea, juice, chocolate and wine. I was curious to learn about his work and I loved being in the warehouse, looking at the numerous products and their packaging, and sometimes I helped him out too.

By the early summer, James had finished university and moved out of his student house to another place. He told me the piano that Max had played on when I had visited his house the first time was his; he had been given it by Dennis and Freda from church. He asked me if I wanted to have the piano at the house I was living in. I was so glad because I used to play the piano in Hungary but didn't have any opportunity over in Wales, and so James and some friends delivered the extremely heavy and hard-to-manhandle piano to the shared lounge of my home.

There was a week when Eszter and Balint went to Hungary for their annual summer break and at the same time James went on a mountain biking holiday to the French Alps with his old friends from school – a trip that had been arranged some time beforehand. I was quite sad to be left on my own for a week without my friends and my boyfriend. During this time, I composed music on the piano and really enjoyed the fact that at least I had something to do to keep me busy during my free time. In addition, James gave me lots of work to do; I had to do all the mailing for his business and my room was full of boxes of leaflets, posters and envelopes, and his printer. I could hardly make a path through my room from one side to the other! We kept in touch online to check I was doing everything correctly.

One afternoon while James was away, I was clearing the weeds from the front of the house and the church worker who taught the English lessons, Jimmy, came by to ask how much I knew about God.

"Hardly anything," I admitted, so he invited me for a chat.

At that point I felt again that God wanted to communicate with me. I went inside to wash my hands quickly and then ran across the road into church to have a conversation. We sat down and he put a piece of paper in front of me that had a diagram explaining the gulf between sinful man and God, which is bridged or made right by the cross. I was in shock, wondering how I could get on the right path to God. He gave me a little book that was written in Hungarian about how to know Jesus and on the back was a prayer. Jimmy said that if I wanted to have God in my life, then in a quiet time I could just say this prayer and God would come into my life:

Lord Jesus Christ,

I am sorry for the things I have done wrong in my life [take a few minutes to ask his forgiveness for anything particular that is on your conscience]. Please forgive me. I now turn from everything that I know is wrong.

Thank you that you died on the cross for me so that I could be forgiven and set free.

Thank you that you offer me forgiveness and the gift of your Spirit. I now receive that gift.

Please come into my life by your Holy Spirit to be with me forever. Thank you, Lord Jesus.

Amen.[7]

Jimmy didn't push me; he just answered my questions and tried to explain about God, but it was hard with the language barrier and my poor English. I still wanted to know more. He said that when I was ready I could be baptised if I wanted to make a public declaration of what I believe, but I declined his offer because I had already been christened as a baby and I thought that baptism should be just once in a lifetime. Then I went home and later that evening I prayed – again, a big step in my life as I didn't pray very often. I prayed for Eszter and Balint to have a safe journey and a good holiday, and for James as well. I was thinking of James a lot and about his faith. Finally, I said the prayer that was written in the book from Jimmy. I found myself crying at that point and felt a warm, peaceful feeling inside of me.

I knew God was with me again.

You call me out upon the waters
The great unknown where feet may fail
And there I find You in the mystery
In oceans deep
My faith will stand [8]

---

[7] From 'Why Jesus' by Nicky Gumbel.
[8] From 'Oceans' by Hillsong, used by permission; see page 131 for the full lyrics.

A little later that evening, I phoned James in France to tell him. He said he wished he was with me and wanted to hug me, and said he was so happy for me.

I knew at some level I now believed in God but I wanted evidence, to see that he was real, to see things with my own eyes. James went to a Bible study home group every week and I was interested too, so I asked Freda if she could help me study the Bible. She happily agreed and for a while we met up once a week in the daytime on my day off.

James came home and we were overjoyed to see each other again.

At the end of August, we travelled to Hungary together. I was quite excited because it was the first time James would be meeting anyone from my family. One of my many cousins, Karesz, picked us up from Budapest Airport and drove us home to my village, a journey of just over two hours, mostly on the motorway. We arrived home, and it was nice and warm there. Because James is vegetarian, my mum had put much effort into cooking special food for him. Then my dad came in with some Palinka, a popular Hungarian fruit brandy, to celebrate that they would use the second person familiar form, not second person formal.[9] This meant a lot to me as it felt like James was starting to become part of my family. We talked for hours around the table but it was very difficult for James as the conservation was all in Hungarian. On the other hand, at least now he knew how hard it was for me in the UK.

The next day we went swimming in the lake, Holt Tisza, where as a child we always spent our very hot summers. We paddled the boat from near my house down to the beach. I really enjoyed this but James isn't as confident in water as me and he was also struggling with the mosquitos – they loved his white, not-at-all-tanned skin. In fact, not just the mosquitos but *everyone* could identify him as a foreigner because of his white skin, and when they found out his name was James they called him James Bond. We had a really fun day and I felt happy that my family were pleased for me.

In the village, my family and our close neighbours used to get together most Saturday evenings for a bit of outdoor cooking and to have a beer or two. On the weekend we arrived it was my parents' turn to host and there were lots of people to meet. Everyone was very

---

[9] like in French, using tu instead of vous

interested because an Englishman was in the village! They asked him what his favourite food was because they wanted to know what food was like in the UK. When he said he was vegetarian, people were surprised because vegetarianism is very rare in Hungary; in fact, I don't know *anyone* Hungarian who is vegetarian.

James was quite confused about who was who because there were so many people there. He couldn't wait for everyone to leave so he could spend some time alone with me and my family, and talk to me in English.

My dad used to be in a band where he played drums. He knew a few old English songs, mainly from The Beatles, and he tried to use some words that he knew from these songs mixed with the few German words he also knew to communicate with James – this was very entertaining to watch. James struggled with my dad's poor accent and the languages! My mum spoke only in Hungarian to James but thought carefully to use basic words and talk slowly, repeating everything without fail, and he understood her quite well. This was in contrast to others around us who didn't seem to make any allowances when speaking to him.

A few days later we left my village and went to Budapest to stay with my older brother Matyi for two nights before our return flight home. I took James round Budapest, showing him some of the sights. He really liked the city but found it difficult to cope with the heat.

Back in the UK, at the end of November I celebrated my 'name day'[10] with a party. James and I had been together for nine months by this time and he had a surprise weekend away planned. He had even contacted my boss secretly to ask for the Friday and Monday off work, which she had agreed to. During the packing, James told me I couldn't take shampoo; I asked why and he told me it was because we would be flying, but he wouldn't tell me where. At Bristol Airport we were asked by security where we were going and why; James had said, "Just say you're going on holiday." I saw on my boarding pass it said "Shannon" but I had no idea where this was. I guessed we were going to Hungary. There was a giant map on the wall showing destinations and I tried to search for Shannon but I couldn't find it.

---

[10] This is a widespread tradition in Hungary and some other European countries, in which everyone with the same name celebrates on a nominated day.

Then, when we sat on the plane, I asked how long we would be flying for because I don't like long flights. James said, "Fifty-seven minutes." So... I now knew we weren't going to Hungary. He then announced that we would be going to Ireland. I had never been there before and neither had he. My English had improved now too so I would be able to understand a bit more.

On the flight, James was studying the "Learn Hungarian" book I had bought him a few months back, and I noticed he was reading the same page for the whole flight. I assumed he was practising the alphabet (which incidentally has forty-two letters so is a bit more complicated than the English alphabet).

He hired a little car from the airport and we drove to Limerick for lunch before driving on for a few hours to a little bed and breakfast, a lovely old cottage in the middle of nowhere on the Dingle peninsula, where we arrived in the dark. The lady owner showed us to our room, where I found three sunflowers in a vase – my favourite flowers! I wondered how they had got there as it was the end of November! Later I found out that James had been in touch to ask them to buy some sunflowers to make a lovely surprise. We partially unpacked and then sat in the lounge by the crackling fire.

Somehow we got on to the topic of engagement. All of my colleagues had said, "Oh, he's going to propose to you," and the fact that he had arranged my days off in secret with my boss made me wonder. I had said to my boss, "I don't want to take days off; just let me work," but she had replied, "No, no, enjoy your weekend."

I said to James, "If ever you want to ask me to get married, don't do anything special, and I don't want a ring because I really hate wearing jewellery." James went strangely quiet...

But it was getting late and we went to bed.

The next day, when I woke up, James was already in the shower. I opened the floor-length curtains by the French doors in the bedroom and saw a huge mountain at the end of the garden! There was a light dusting of snow on the ridge.

"Have you seen this?" I shouted. "Did you know? You've got to come and see this!"

In turned out that James had specially chosen this place.

We enjoyed a nice breakfast, packed our things and went out to the car. It was very cold though and James had to ask the bed and breakfast owners for an ice scraper to clear the windscreen because there wasn't one in the hire car. I stood by the vehicle, freezing cold, while he removed the ice.

After a few minutes of driving, we had warmed up nicely and during the journey we were delighted with how scenic and beautiful the area was. We took a right turn on to a narrow road and drove up to park just before a gate at the end of the lane, which was by a lake and surrounded by mountains.

James asked me if I fancied a little walk. It was extremely cold but in spite of this I agreed. I needed to wear his jumper around my head, just to keep a bit warmer. We walked for about five minutes before turning around and walking back towards the car as it was so chilly. Then, as we stopped by the lake for a moment, James suddenly started singing! He sang a famous Hungarian song called "Tavaszi Szel", which is a special song for me because it's about "Virág"[11].

I said, "Wow, that's nice, you learned the whole song in Hungarian."

He went on to say in Hungarian how important I was to him, and that he really wanted me in his life so much, then he dropped to one knee and switched to English to ask, "Will you marry me?"

The smile on my face was beaming as I replied, "I will!"

I was shaking because of the cold and had James' old jumper around my head – very attractive! We kissed and hugged each other in great happiness, and neither of us could really believe what had just happened. We smiled so much! The rest of the day was spent enjoying good food and breathtaking scenery, and sharing the news with friends and family by phone, text message and social media.

The rest of the holiday was a road trip across Ireland, including meeting a Hungarian friend in Cork, followed by a ferry back to Wales. I found out later that part of the reason James had sold his car a few weeks earlier was to pay for this "engagement holiday".

Soon after I felt I needed to speak to James about how strongly I wanted us to live together before we got married; to see his days and nights and to know what to expect. He was a bit unsure about this but after a while he agreed that this would help us get to know one other better; we had only been together nine months and it was still

---

[11] 'Virág' means 'flower' in Hungarian

an early relationship, although we knew we really loved each other. We found a property to rent and I loved spending time at our new home with James and the feeling of waiting for him to come home from work. I was no longer alone.

There were some days when I still struggled that we weren't more 'physical' but I realised how important this issue was for James and in this way I started to know him a bit better. I wanted to learn more about his Christian faith and to understand what the Bible says. So we started to plan our wedding which we decided would take place eleven months later in October 2010. My parents helped a lot with the preparations.

During our engagement we went to Hungary twice for a week at a time – in January and in June. In my village we have a French-style fairy-tale castle which was an important part of my childhood. Almost all girls from the village get married there and since a young age I had always dreamed of having my wedding there too. But then we were informed that we couldn't use the castle because it was going to be undergoing a major renovation that would last over a year, so we had to search for a 'Plan B'. There is a large cottage in the village that operates as self-catering accommodation and has a wine cellar that is used for events. This became the new wedding destination.

The wedding preparation was not without stress, especially concerning the guest list – how many people we could accommodate, and of course who. We had always thought of having the wedding in Hungary, never in the UK. We didn't want to have a big wedding, only to celebrate with people that were important in our life, people whom we were sure we would keep in touch with over the years.

We both wanted to get married in church, but in Hungary you have to have a civil ceremony for the legal aspect of the wedding, which is usually held at the registry office or council village hall. During our next visit in June we went to have a chat with the registrar about our plan. We told her that we would like our wedding on October 2nd and that if she would be able to come to the cottage, that would be great as the church was just across the road from it. Traditionally you get the legal ceremony completed first but we wanted God's blessing first and to get married in God's eyes, then to rush through the civil ceremony with the bare minimum. The registrar informed us that we would need to gather a number of documents – proof of identity for our witnesses, a translation of James' birth certificate and all his documents – and then she would have to send our application to the county office. They would decide within a month whether they approved of our marriage and the day we'd chosen.

Mum and I went to see some wedding dresses. I had already chosen the bridesmaids' dresses for two important little girls with my sister-in-law, Haze. But although I tried a number of wedding dresses on, I didn't feel happy with any of them. Eventually, however, the right one was found. As I tried it on and looked in the mirror, I couldn't stay composed; the dress was beautiful and I found myself in tears. We were told that it was a new design that had come from England. "Wow!" I joked. "So we are having a British wedding after all, then!" In Hungary people hire the wedding dress rather than buy. So I had the dress fitted and I bought a pair of shoes to go with it, plus some accessories.

There are various Hungarian wedding traditions, but we decided our wedding would be a mix of Hungarian and British traditions. For example, there is a tradition that the bride changes out of her wedding dress at midnight into a red dress and dances with everyone, who need to give her money, until the groom comes back to 'steal' his wife. We didn't want to include this even though it's traditional because I wasn't comfortable about receiving all the money from people. A wedding is not about money and I knew some of the family would find it financially difficult, so we didn't want them to give us presents either. But of course you can't tell this to family – and even if you did, they wouldn't listen. The shop assistant included the midnight dress in the price of the wedding dress but I didn't want it. So I left the shop with instructions regarding the collection of the dress before the wedding.

Over the previous few weeks, several emails had been exchanged with the priest about the service and we told him we wanted it to be in both English and Hungarian. He was happy to take the service in both languages. While we were in Hungary we went to visit the priest, to discuss everything in more detail. We translated the entire service to create a bilingual service booklet so nobody would miss out, and also translated the words spoken in the registrar's service afterwards, which would be entirely in Hungarian.

I made the invitation cards – something I really enjoyed – and James wrote a useful guide of instructions for the British guests about the long weekend that they would spend in Hungary for the wedding.

Mum and Dad organised a lot for us – such as the catering, which took them lot of time – and one of my aunts, Lili, offered to make the table decorations.

Then one day we received a phone call saying that we could actually have the wedding at the castle, but we would in fact be the last couple to use the castle before it closed for the major renovations. We were so happy; although we had already sent the wedding invitations stating the reception would be held elsewhere, it would be in the same village with everything close by, so it didn't matter. We still hadn't heard any news from the council regarding the permission to marry, but the village registrar assured us that we would get the permission in time.

Towards the end of September, James and I became very excited. James' van driver came with us to Bristol Airport. James drove there and Martin took the vehicle back. He was late and this added to our stress levels somewhat as we stood on the pavement outside our apartment waiting for him. We were leaving the UK as an engaged young couple and looked forward to our big day in Hungary.

We arrived in Tiszadob just over a week before the wedding with a lot to do. The coming days included various trips to buy all the food, drink, and special wines needed for the wedding as we were organising all the catering ourselves. It was fun calculating how much of everything we needed, choosing which wine to buy, and so on. We also visited the priest again and had a practice wedding service, and we needed to check if James understood everything and could give all the right responses.

Our lovely neighbour and friends from the village went with Mum and me to help to decorate the rooms of the castle where we would hold the reception, and also to wash and dry all the glasses, cutlery and crockery as they had accrued dust and dirt, lying unused for a while.

After we'd completed most of our work, the girls organised a kind of surprise hen party for me, which I hadn't expected, and because I had been so busy I hadn't planned one and didn't think I would have one at all. But I was really happy that they had thought of me. I had to put on an old traditional dress and jewellery, and I needed to complete lots of challenges like picking up money from the floor and dancing, then they gave me a certificate that said I can get married. We had so much fun and I was thankful that everyone helped us.

Just two days before the wedding, we received the news from the Village Council that we could officially get married. I couldn't believe that it had come at the last minute and wondered why it had taken so many months for the approval. The registrar simply remarked that the administrator had gone on holiday and handed over our paperwork to a colleague but nothing had happened with it until her return. We had already put together a backup plan as it had been unclear whether the legal go-ahead would be granted in time. The plan was that we would still have the church service and reception to celebrate the wedding on the day in Hungary with our friends and family, and then when we got back to the UK after our honeymoon we would get legally married. After all, it was the church service – getting married in God's eyes – that was important, not the legal difference between a Hungarian and British church wedding. The registrar agreed to come to the castle after the church service to complete her part of our wedding.

My brother Matyi went to the airport to meet and greet a lot of the British guests who were landing on Thursday evening, and helped them get into the city by train. They had made their own arrangements for accommodation and sightseeing the next morning.

That evening we spent many hours, late into the evening, printing out the seating plan, place names, menu and service sheets. It was quite fun, albeit a little stressful being so last minute.

The next day, the day before the wedding, Dad went to the city to collect my flowers and dress. James cooked a vegetarian soup for the starter, the way he wanted it, as British soup is quite a different affair from Hungarian soup. The latter is served out watery, to which everyone adds chicken, vegetable chunks and homemade pasta twirls to their own bowl in whatever proportion they choose.

Most of the twenty-five or so guests who'd travelled from the UK for the wedding arrived in the afternoon. We had booked taxis to bring them from the centre of Budapest to the village, and whilst everyone got to the rendezvous point, a major train station, with my brother Matyi on time, the taxis were two hours late arriving as they couldn't find the train station, so unfortunately our guests had rather a boring wait.

Some of James' family avoided this as they didn't want to make the motorway journey, so had chosen to travel by train to Miskolc, from where Dad and a neighbour had driven to collect them. Neither Dad nor the neighbour speak English, but somehow they found each other and got back to the village without difficulty. Max and his girlfriend arrived later in the evening with two of my cousins as they'd got a late flight on the Friday.

Most of the British guests were staying in the cottage; but there are only six rooms so we'd booked a couple of nearby bed and breakfasts for others. We welcomed them with a glass of Hungarian Palinka all round and served dinner for everyone. After they had all settled in and had their dinner, James and the guys went out for his 'stag do' of sorts.

My friend Eszter was my witness, a role more important in Hungary than the UK, and she and her husband Balint were staying at my neighbour's bed and breakfast. That evening, because Balint was out with the guys and Eszter didn't want to be alone in the house, I went with her and chatted all night until Balint came back very late in the morning. I hardly slept as it was so cold in the room.

I needed to get ready for the hairdresser. We went to see her really early with Eszter and later Dad popped over with breakfast for us. The hairdresser started with Eszter's hair, which took ages, and all of a sudden we had almost run out of time; there was hardly any time to do *my* hair. The wedding was at one o'clock but we only finished at the hairdresser at half past twelve. It was such a rush to quickly put on my dress and brush my teeth, but I made it – just about.

I took my lovely bouquet – sunflowers, of course – and waited with Dad, the priest and the bridesmaids by the entrance to the church. Everyone else was already inside.

I felt so nervous but was excited at the same time. We had chosen a nice song for me to walk down the aisle, which someone sang solo and unaccompanied from the gallery. I glanced at James standing at the front of the church waiting for me and became even more nervous. I couldn't wait to see him properly. When I got to the end of the aisle, Dad kissed my cheek as he left me. James and I immediately took each other's hands and held them tightly, and James told me I looked beautiful.

The priest welcomed everyone in both English and Hungarian, then we went through the ceremony and we made our promises before God, exchanged our rings, and of course finally kissed each other.

After the service we went out of the church and everyone came out after us to congratulate and kiss our cheeks; this is the tradition. I had an additional bouquet made up and I threw it over my shoulder, but when I turned around I saw that nobody caught it. Dad threw it back to me to have another throw and this time it landed in my childhood friend Katika's hand (but she hasn't got married yet, five years on).

It was then time to make our way to the castle for the second ceremony and reception. We led a procession of everyone walking from the church, which was about a ten-minute walk. It was difficult for James walking alongside me not to step on my dress whilst walking close enough to hold my hand. People came out of their houses to congratulate us. Then as we got to the castle, the registrar was waiting for us for the next service, and as people took their seats, James' best man Max played some gentle background music on the guitar. We had asked my cousin's son, who speaks fluent English, to read the translation that we had prepared so that the English-speaking guests could understand. Now, at last, we were officially and legally married! We celebrated with champagne. Our friends and family began the large buffet as a kind of late lunch while James and I went outside into the castle grounds to have some photographs taken. We had lovely autumn-coloured photographs outside the castle, around the park and by the river.

When we got back to the castle the band had started to play and people were dancing, but we saved ourselves for later. The English guests were nowhere to be seen and we later found out they'd all gone back to their accommodation – for some reason they assumed the reception wasn't until evening. A while later we opened the door into the dining room for dinner and everyone took a welcome drink – such as a glass of Palinka, cream brandy or vodka amongst others. We had thought carefully to place Hungarians who could speak

English near English guests, along with the usual considerations, and it worked quite well.

James stood up and started his speech. Everyone was amazed when he spoke in both languages and all I could think about was how blessed I was to have him in my life. Then Max did the best man's speech and everyone applauded. We ate our lovely dinner and then after most of the guests were dancing we joined in too. Because we had been busy with the wedding preparations in the preceding week, we had skipped celebrating Dad's birthday, which was a few days before the wedding. So as a birthday surprise for him, James and I sang one of his favourite songs from The Beatles, and then I danced with him. It was a special and touching time.

We had such a fun wedding, being together with the most important people in our life.

The next day family and friends helped us to clear out everything and we were off to our honeymoon in Italy. We spent five or six lovely days in a coastal village in Puglia and then two days in Rome. As there was so much left over, we managed to take one of the four wedding cakes to Italy.

My facial recognition memory is very good. At Budapest Airport I had seen a couple in the departure lounge and then when we arrived at Bari I saw them again at the car hire when James was collecting our car. It was a big surprise to see this couple once again a few days later as we were looking around the town of Lecce, especially as it was a few hours' drive from the airport we'd both flown into. I recognised them straightaway and heard them speaking Hungarian to each other.

"That's the couple from the airport," I said to James.

He encouraged me to go and say hello so I went over and commented that I had heard them speaking Hungarian and had seen them at the airport. "Are you on holiday or visiting family?" I asked.

It turned out that the woman, Katalin, was a Hungarian organist who had travelled over to Italy to do an organ recital a few days later. We ended up having a coffee together and started to chat more, and I told them we were on our honeymoon and had just got married. We discovered they were a Christian couple, and they explained it was also a kind of honeymoon for them as they had three children but had left them at home so that they could concentrate on each other. It turned out that they couldn't hire the car that they had booked because they didn't have a credit card for the deposit. We offered to take them on a day trip together one day to go to the southern tip of Puglia, where they wanted to go and which we had also planned on visiting, so a few days later they came with us in our tiny Citroen C1 hire car. Afterward, Katalin invited us to her concert recital and we said we would attend. That evening we went to the church and listened to her play the organ for a while but for some reason it wasn't working properly. So to compensate the audience she decided to sing in Hungarian. It was lovely and very emotional for me, and must have been quite a rare event for someone in Italy to be singing a performance in Hungarian. We were so glad to have met them and got to know them, and we promised to try to keep in touch, hoping to see each other again one day.

CHAPTER FOUR

Life as a Married Couple
and Moving to Bath

The Lord ... blesses the home of the upright.

Proverbs 3:33

When we came back to the UK, I thought it was a dream, but to see James with me every day was *more* than a dream. I started to believe God had a plan for me and that he wanted James in my life so that I could get to know him more. He was using people around me to reach him; I felt he was working hard on me.

I am so grateful to have James. He opened my eyes and we started talking about God a bit more. However, sometimes I got confused and had questions like, why is this or that happening?

By this time, my younger brother Bence had finished school in Hungary and didn't know what he wanted to do, so we invited him to stay at our home for a while and learn English too. On our next visit to Hungary in January, three months after getting married, he flew back with us to start his new life in the UK. He started off doing a few hours' work with James in the warehouse but there wasn't enough to do. It was difficult finding a job with his limited English but he found some work delivering magazines and leaflets and cutting people's lawns. He also joined a football club. We had plenty of precious times together and it felt like we had a child. But the downside was when we came home from work and he hadn't washed up or cooked anything for us. That was just my lovely, lazy brother!

He felt homesick and didn't feel he wanted to stay in the UK, so after six months he returned to Hungary to move back in with our parents. We felt this was understandable; after all, not everyone can leave their home, family and friends for a long period. When he was gone, we missed him at times, and the house felt empty and strange, so we made an almost life-sized cardboard cut-out of him to put in the lounge.

I had been working in the care home for three years and I wasn't happy anymore. I didn't feel anyone appreciated my work. It wasn't easy to work with old people with dementia. I enjoyed it and I loved caring for them, but I felt they wanted more. Over the time I worked there, I met lots of family members who *did* appreciate me and thanked me for organising activities for the residents, something to fill their days. I was now working on the Activities Team, with two others, and we sometimes took the residents out of the care home for a walk or for lunch somewhere. We also encouraged a lot of reminiscing by showing old films which they often remembered, listening to old popular music, and talking about the past with them. This was all in addition to running bingo and quizzes, holding birthday celebrations, knitting, nail colouring, and sometimes a bit of light dancing. They loved bingo and I loved playing it with them. I found it really funny how all of the numbers have special bingo names, like "two fat ladies".

James was going through a tough time as well. He had transferred his business to a joint venture with someone else, but this ended up going wrong for him and the outcome was that the other partner took over the business and James was left with nothing; as if it had been stolen from him. I felt angry because James had given up his other job to concentrate on this business and immediately he had lost it for good. I felt so sorry for him; he didn't deserve this. He is such a good man who was doing his work to help others.

So we decided to move and start a new chapter in our lives together. Although we were living in Cardiff, James is English and he missed his home country so we planned to move away. He started searching for jobs and when he found one in Bath as a mortgage advisor, I started looking for jobs there too. We had visited James' friends in Bath once and I had loved it from the first. I read about how famous it was, and to me it felt more like being in Italy than England. So unique. Soon James spotted an advertisement for an ideal job for me. Straightaway I got an interview in a nursery as a cook. I felt this would be a good step closer to working with children, which is what I was really keen to do. The interview went well and I got the job and had to start in one week's time. I told my boss at the care home, worked a final couple of days and used my accrued holiday to cover the rest of my notice period.

As it all happened so suddenly, we had to find our new home quickly. My job was starting one week before James' was due to start. For my first week, I commuted from Cardiff by train. We found a flat as well but couldn't move in as, rather frustratingly, the current occupier was delayed in moving out. For my second week at work and James' starting week, James found us somewhere to stay with a family, a little outside of Bath. So we stayed there from Sunday until Friday and then, with Eszter and Balint's help in packing up our home, we moved to Bath by van at the weekend. It was hard to leave them but I knew our friendship wasn't over, and anyway, Cardiff isn't far so we looked forward to seeing each other again soon. We also phoned each other every week and I talked with Eszter for hours on the phone; and when we met there was still ample to talk about. We can always restart our conversations where we left off last time!

I never ever imagined that I would have a job where I would need to cook for forty children! But they really enjoyed my food and I made new healthy menus for each term, even putting a delicious Hungarian recipe in there as well: courgette bake. The children started to talk to me and I happily chatted with them.

Shortly after we moved to Bath, my older brother Matyi and his fiancée, who were expecting their baby daughter, moved to the same town from Budapest.

After trying a few churches, James settled on one that was nearby and we started to go to the services. When I first went I felt full of peace and the people there were really friendly. There were lots of families with children, and people of all ages. Over the coming weeks and months, we started to talk to more people. Patrick, the rector, and his wife Olivia held a newcomers' supper so we went along to introduce ourselves and to meet others who had recently started going to the church. We enjoyed a lovely evening with them.

Every two to three years, the church organises a trip to Lee Abbey, a Christian conference and retreat centre in Devon, and after we'd been attending a while, we saw this special weekend advertised in the weekly newssheet. We decided to join them. We didn't have a car at that time but the weekend's organisers arranged a lift for us with a couple we hadn't met before – Mandy and Paul. We travelled with them for the three-hour journey and talked almost the entire way, as well as listening to and discussing their music with them, and our friendship was born. Mandy and Paul are such an amazing couple in our life. We had a lovely time at Lee Abbey and I also met some young Hungarians who were serving in the community. It is a very special place.

I enjoyed cooking but it wasn't a big enough challenge for me. I asked my manager if I could be more involved with the children, perhaps helping in the afternoon at snack time with feeding them, washing their hands or being in the room to play with them. Luckily, she said yes. Then I reached the realisation that this is what I always wanted to do: to be a nursery nurse, to help the children develop their communication skills, have fun and play with them.

After eight months of cooking, my manager offered me a job as a nursery assistant. I was so happy and couldn't wait to start my on-the-job NVQ course to become a nursery nurse. My brother wasn't happy at his workplace and it seemed like good timing for him to change jobs as well so I asked if he could be interviewed for the cooking job I was leaving. He successfully passed the interview and so we ended up working at the same place. I enjoyed being with the children, whatever activities we did with them – playing out in the garden, going for a walk around town, or to the park to watch the trains. And of course there were lots of activities inside as well. I got to know them more as individuals and engaged with their parents as well when they dropped off and collected their children.

"I am so happy," I thought to myself. "I have an amazing husband, I live where I feel it's home and I'm doing what I always wanted to do."

Around this time my niece was born. She was beautiful and I was so proud to be her auntie. I went to see her after work and at weekends and started to treat her with clothes and toys. I enjoyed all my cuddles with her. When she was three months old, my brother and his fiancée needed to go to the Hungarian Embassy in London to obtain a Hungarian passport for her and I looked after her all day. I took her to nursery while I was working, but because she was younger than the children I was with, she was in a different room from me. I could hear when she was crying, and now and then I popped round to see her. She was always really happy to see me. She was usually just crying because she was hungry; she always liked getting her milk bottle.

I enjoyed doing my course and I couldn't believe I was studying in English. I had a kind and supportive tutor who helped me when I couldn't understand something immediately. But I had a lot of homework so I was with my books at home whenever possible.

CHAPTER FIVE

Starting a Family

Through each day the Lord pours his unfailing love upon me, and through each night I sing his songs, praying to God who gives me life.

Psalm 42:8

How could we improve our lives even more? How could we feel even more fulfilled and complete? By growing our family, by having a child. We were already very happy in Bath and I took pleasure from my job. We felt we wanted to fill our life with even more happiness and joy. I was sure that God wanted that too.

In August 2012 I became pregnant. We were so thrilled. I couldn't wait to tell my parents so we had a Skype video call and I said, "Your grandchild is on the way!"

I had already booked to fly to Hungary in September but this time I was going on my own, and it was strange to be travelling without James. Because it was going to be our first wedding anniversary soon, we came up with a plan to meet in Paris for a city break after I'd been to Hungary. James was to travel from Bath by train to London and then by coach to Paris through the night, arriving early in the morning. I enjoyed being with my parents for a few days, talking about my pregnancy and eating some delicious Hungarian food.

Naturally, I suffered all the usual pregnancy symptoms, feeling sick and tired much of the time, and most of the night I was awake. I looked forward to seeing James but during the flight to Paris I felt so sick that I had my eyes closed for almost the entire flight.

Charles de Gaulle airport in Paris was so big that I thought I would never find my way through so many people! But eventually I spotted James and it was the best feeling ever. We agreed, "Let's not be apart from each other for such a long time again." It had been less than a week!

We had an amazing time in Paris. We did the usual sightseeing: museums and famous places. We didn't go up the Eiffel Tower; I was already feeling dizzy and sick, but when we saw the queue, that made the decision for us. We carried on walking and enjoying other sights instead.

When we arrived back home we had an appointment for the first ultrasound scan. It was so exciting to see our baby on the big monitor – an amazing and very emotional experience. James held my hands tightly, firmly, and I simply couldn't believe how tiny this child in me could be – at the time of the scan, only six centimetres long. We saw the heart and the brain, and the baby amused us by opening and closing his hand as if he was waving to us. When I put one of my hands behind my back, he did the same – as though he could see and copy me! We got pictures of the baby and I put one in a frame.

They couldn't tell us the child's gender yet – we needed to wait until the twenty-week scan for that – but I felt straightaway when I saw the scan that he was a boy. James was not convinced, but the voice that had guided me so often in life spoke over and over again: "Luki. Luki."

During this time, I was eager to learn and follow how the baby was growing in me, what he was doing and how he was developing, so we got a large hardback "Pregnant Body" book which detailed everything that was happening week by week throughout the pregnancy.

Soon I was into my second trimester and I started to write a "Bump to Birth" journal about what had happened so far, and then each week. It was so exciting to write in it every day how I felt and how I was putting on weight. We had an appointment to hear the baby's heart, which was another emotional moment. When I read the information in my journal, it said that by this week the baby's approximate size was that of an avocado, so I played in my mind with fruit and vegetable sizes each week.

Soon afterwards I started to feel the baby. It was an unusual, sometimes tickly feeling. I called him Luki secretly. When I asked him if he liked this name, he answered with a kick! I enjoyed all his movements.

We had busy days at work and weren't happy with where we lived, a basement flat, as it was dark and we had a lot of mould there. We wanted to move for our and the baby's health and also because there were steps down to our flat which would have been difficult to handle with a pushchair. So James' friends and my brother helped us to move to a better place in the same area, close to the hospital and church.

Then we had the twenty-week scan to find out how the baby was doing and the gender – is he Luke or not? The baby was estimated at 295 grams, and was sleeping with his hands on his face. At first the sonographer had difficulty identifying the gender from the image, but then she found what she was looking for and announced, "I can see his snail." I cried because it was a relief; we really wanted a boy. James was happy too and admitted I had been right. He was also happy with the name Luke, but we didn't tell anyone else.

We enjoyed a pre-Christmas meal with James' sister and brother at our home, by which time my pregnancy was already visible. My brother, his then girlfriend and their daughter (my lovely niece), and our friends Eszter and Balint also came from Cardiff for a pre-Christmas meal.

Between those visits we had another scan to check if everything was progressing fine. Luke's face wasn't covered this time; he rubbed his eyes instead and blew bubbles through his mouth. He was very active, weighed 513 grams and was the same size as a papaya.

From this time on, I started to feel quite uncomfortable, especially when sitting down, and I had heartburn and didn't sleep well. I hoped

I wouldn't suffer the same way all through the pregnancy because I didn't want to be exhausted after the birth. We had a busy Christmas, going to Devon on the train and staying with James' mum, and a few days later staying with his dad.

Then we were off to Hungary for the New Year. Already people could see my little 'bump' and everyone seemed to share in our excitement. Our baby seemed excited too; he was so active there. We went to look at baby products in a few shops with my parents, just to see what was available in Hungary, but we decided to get most of it in the UK. It was hard to go back to work upon our return; we had spent some lovely days with my family.

I was enjoying my pregnancy and at this point I read that the baby could hear now, so I just talked a lot with my Luki and played on the piano, which he enjoyed. Also he enjoyed the times in church when we were singing worship songs. I couldn't see him but he was already with us and so became part of our little family.

Then before I knew it, I was into the third trimester and I had a scan again to see how everything was going. Luki seemed very comfortable and was smiling. I couldn't believe he already weighed about a kilo and how he was just squashed up inside me. My weight went up normally as well and I experienced cravings. I needed to have 'Anti D' because of my blood type and with the baby's blood type being unknown. From this point I cut my hours at work.

At pregnancy week thirty James and I celebrated our fourth anniversary (of being together, not marriage) and also my brother's thirtieth birthday and my niece's first. I was babysitting at the Priory Hotel for the whole weekend and helped out with the baby group on Sunday during the service. It was a busy but exciting week.

From then on we started to buy baby products. We bought the cot and some clothes, and it began to sink in that the baby was really coming!

I worked my last week at the nursery and had my first parent meeting too. It went well. I had begun to find it difficult to lift the children up and bend my back all the time so it was time to say goodbye. I had a fantastic week at the nursery, in which I also celebrated my birthday. I received lots of cards and presents, and the children sang to me.

I enjoyed my maternity leave and found myself just looking at Luke's clothes for long periods of time. I had my last scan appointment and everything was fine. They did comment that Luke's head was a bit bigger than normal but added that I didn't need to worry about it. So I was not worried.

One day I received a delivery – a lovely flower bouquet from one of the parents at the nursery to say thank you for looking after their child. I felt really touched and we kept in contact with one another; the family didn't live far from us. And I kept in contact with another family too, who lived on the other side of town.

I had a lovely Easter but also some sad days. My dad's cousin died and it was hard not to be at home with the extended family. I cried a lot but didn't want to cause stress for the baby. So it was difficult to cope. James still wasn't enjoying his work and had some interviews elsewhere, but without success. I just wished for him to be happier. Mum came over for a fortnight to help and arrived the day before the due date; we didn't expect him to come early. So we had a nice time together. I started to feel less like myself and more like a spoilt, grumpy child, saying, "I don't want to do this. I don't want to do that." I hardly slept and I just moaned a lot.

I was waiting for my appointment for Monday, to be induced, but on Saturday I felt odd and my water seemed to be leaking. So we decided it was best to check with the hospital. James called Mandy who had offered to take us there at any time since we didn't have a car ourselves. Bless her, it was her husband Paul's birthday and we had just disturbed them. But she didn't mind and was happy and excited for me.

After we arrived at hospital I started to have a little pain and it became noticeably more regular. I wasn't fully dilated so I had to go to a room to wait for the natural onset of my labour. It wasn't an easy night, I hardly ate anything and I just squeezed James' hands every two to five minutes or so. Early Sunday morning we went down to the delivery room as I had so much pain and felt I had to push. James called Mum, who arrived very quickly, and the big work started. I had gas and air and tried to change my position as it was so difficult to lie on the bed. They sent me to the toilet which was very difficult for me; then they remembered I wanted a water birth but I wasn't strong enough to come out of the bed again. At about one o'clock I started to push for one-and-a-half hours but nothing really happened. James and Mum helped me to drink enough water and they wetted my face. They were amazing! I was in so much pain.

Twice they tried to turn Luke's head in me, as he was rotated ninety degrees round the wrong way. But then they decided to take me to the theatre and have a forceps delivery as his heart rate had started to slow down. The plan was, if that didn't work then I would have to have a caesarean section. I was worried and asked, "Why didn't they do anything earlier?" but of course it's their job and I trusted they knew what to do.

James came into the theatre with me and Mum waited outside. I asked him to pray for me and for it all to go well. I had a spinal anaesthetic so I couldn't feel anything from the bottom of my back downwards. I held his hand tightly and I had to push but I couldn't feel anything due to the anaesthetic. On the third push I saw the doctor taking the baby out and the nurses took him away from us to make sure that he was fine.

Luke didn't cry at first and needed some rescue breaths. I felt bad that I couldn't see him straightaway. But James reassured me that he would be fine. Then finally they put him on my chest, wrapped in towels, and I welcomed him to this world. When I looked at him I remarked that he looked like a miniature version of my maternal grandad – precisely the same. James kissed me and said he was so proud of me. One of the nurses asked what his name was and we could finally announce he was called Luke.

Luke weighed 3.57kg[12] and was fifty-three centimetres long. The nurses gave him to James and the two of them needed to go out. James didn't know what to do, but I said, "Just hold him as he is now and I'll be coming soon." I had to stay in theatre for them to sew me back up and make sure I was OK, then they pushed me through to where James and Luke were waiting for me. I suddenly felt dizzy, a bit shaky and nauseous. It felt odd that he was not in my womb anymore and I still couldn't feel my legs. Mum came too and kissed me, then she held Luke and couldn't put her smile away.

We were assigned a room and went upstairs. I felt so hot and the nurse came to check if everything was fine. Luke's right eye was shut

---

[12] seven pounds, fourteen ounces

and bruised, as well as his ear, because of the forceps so we wanted to have him checked over. A doctor came to examine him and said that his eye and ear would be red for a few days but he would be fine.

James was amazing; he had packed all kinds of things for me and also food. I put Luke on my chest for the first time to feed him. It was a bit difficult but I just kept trying to get our positions right. It's the most beautiful feeling that a mother and child can have together. I became Luke's mum and I knew I was going to share my life with this tiny little boy and take care of him. I loved every bit of him. His tiny feet, toes, hands...

James received numerous phone calls and I spoke with my dad who cried over the phone. My brother Matyi came to see us later that day and kissed Luke and me. James posted photos on social media, allowing our friends and family to all see the baby.

That night I thanked God for looking after Luke and me, and bringing a beautiful, healthy boy into our lives. Despite being so tired, I couldn't sleep much as I felt too excited. James was allowed to stay one more night with us. He was such a help all night.

The next day we went to a different room where only Luke and I stayed. Eszter and Balint came to visit us in the hospital. Then my mum came and looked after Luke with James while I had a shower. It was really difficult to get up, to walk and to sit but the smile on my face never faded, like when James had proposed to me. There was another new life in my life! To me, Luke was perfect – and very cuddly. His eye and ear recovered but I felt sorry for him. Because my temperature was slightly high and I didn't feel confident to go home yet, I stayed one more night, although this time James wasn't allowed to remain with us. Luke was simply beautiful and I felt like I could watch him all night. He kept waking up through the night because he was so hungry, which was a good introduction to how the following weeks and months were going to be. In the morning James texted me saying, "Good morning, my family, looking forward to taking you two home!" It felt so real; the family was now *three* of us. Then he came and took us on the very short journey home in a taxi. My mum was waiting for us with a lovely lunch and she stayed with us for the rest of the week.

Luke slept for hours and hours. He only really woke up for milk, every two to three hours, and I didn't mind when he woke me in the night. He was amazing. He started to listen to the voices around him and knew who his mummy and daddy were. We held a video call with my dad and my younger brother; it felt almost as though they were with us. Luke's first bath didn't go too well. He cried a lot and really didn't like it. In fact, it took him a long time to get used to his daily wash.

The day after the video call, 'Mama Pam', James' mum, came and shared lots of cuddles with Luke. At one time she changed his nappy and we warned her to be careful because he liked pooing everywhere – and, oh yes, he managed to have a poo on Mama Pam. Then the midwife came from the hospital to see us. He did so well with feeding.

The first week was a blur of visitors every day. James' dad came with his partner Jenny. Luke was lucky to have three grandmas. Then my brother came with my niece, then James' sister with her children and James' brother and sister-in-law.

Everyone was very excited and gave Luke cuddles. For me it was hard to sit as I was in so much pain because of my cut. But James borrowed a special comfortable inflatable cushion for me, which really helped along with my painkillers.

My mum had to go back to Hungary to resume her job, as her annual leave had run out, and James had one more week off from work on paternity leave. I started to worry how I would manage with Luke on my own. In particular, Luke liked his milk but he sucked so quickly and it made him choke each time he fed; it sounded as though he was struggling to breathe. So I needed to work out what to do in these situations.

After a few days we took Luke out for the first time, which was good. However, the first few times we went out, he cried and James began to panic so we had to go back to the house. I needed to calm him down and explain that it was normal, that we just needed to rock the buggy. Another milestone was our first "big trip out", a bus journey to town to register Luke's birth and obtain his birth certificate.

Luke was a good baby. We went to church, where he had his first blessing and the community welcomed him. I felt like he knew where he was. In my tummy he had always been active during the loud worship and now he just listened and smiled when he heard the music and singing. When he was hungry he always let everyone know! When he cried I had to go out of the service into the crèche with him because he was too loud.

At this time, James was helping the church treasurer with financial administration. So he needed to go to the office, and Luke and I went with him to the Church Centre but we went to the small baby group instead, our first time. We met Sarah and her daughter Evelyn who was almost a year old. It was good to know other people, mums from church with their babies. Whenever we could, we met up each week.

As James' paternity leave finished and he went back to work, Luke and I started to find our own routine. When I felt better and Luke was sleeping I decided to continue working on my NVQ on the laptop. Then we went for walks and he enjoyed when I was singing to him. I spoke both English and Hungarian to him, and he enjoyed turning his head to listen to my voice. I loved being his Mummy and enjoyed my maternity leave, finally doing things with him, with my own child, not with other children as I had been doing at the nursery. I thanked God every day for my beautiful boy and his health. Luke had received so many presents and cards so I made thank you cards and posted them when we were walking.

We had a lovely summer and it was wonderful to watch Luke's development. He loved it when he realised he could make noises. I loved it too when he couldn't sleep in the night and we went to the lounge so as not to wake James up and just looked at the road outside our window, brightly illuminated with streetlights, in the early hours of the morning when people staggered home drunk from parties, or lorries stopped outside making deliveries to the shop we lived by. Sometimes in the nights James took Luke out of the bedroom to let me sleep for a while and they had fun together, but – poor James! – he needed to go to work the next day and he was really tired, although of course he enjoyed every minute spent with Luke.

Around this time, my brother's girlfriend left him and we felt very sad for him. We knew it would be difficult for him not seeing his daughter as often.

James had been searching for a new job for ages and finally started one in July, in logistics, which is what he really wanted to do. A few days before he began he realised he would need a car for this job to get around to the various sites, and at the moment we didn't have one. So we spent the weekend looking everywhere for a car and managed to obtain one just in time. James ended up spending several weeks away from Monday to Friday in this new job. I enjoyed hearing his stories when he came home for the weekend. However, it was sometimes difficult when he came home and wanted to be Luke's dad as I had established a routine already and it was difficult to meld the two.

We were planning to go to Hungary so we applied for Luke's passport and it didn't take long to arrive. We looked forward to seeing my parents, especially my dad and younger brother, who hadn't seen Luke for real, just in photos and online video calls.

When the time came in September, we drove to Luton airport the evening before our flight, managing to get most of the way before needing to stop to feed Luke. We stayed in a hotel right at the airport so we were close by for our early start. The flight itself went really well and he slept almost the whole journey. This time we were flying to Debrecen, closer to where my parents live than flying to Budapest. They came to meet us at the airport. It was a lovely feeling and of course very emotional for Dad to meet Luke and for Mum to see him again. And all the family, friends and neighbours were happy for us. Luke enjoyed the atmosphere and cuddles; he seemed happy being with everyone.

My dad was so proud of me and immediately took out pictures of when he was a child. He couldn't stop telling me and everyone else how much Luke looked like him at that age. Of course, I saw the resemblance of lots of family members in Luke. Anyway, we had a lot of fun and enjoyed being in Hungary. Luke met his great-grandparents on my mother's side and it was wonderful to see so many generations together in one room.

After a few days, James had to go back to work, and Luke and I stayed a little longer. As usual, it felt strange to be apart from each other, but we were alright and Luke was amazing with everyone. He tried a bit of apple purée and he really enjoyed it.

Then the day arrived when we had to go back. My parents and Bence took us to Budapest airport but before the flight we were able to meet with my niece briefly, whom I hadn't seen for several months due to her parents' separation. It was nice to have that opportunity and she enjoyed spending the short time with us. The separation had been painful for all of us, and particularly so for my parents who had a granddaughter whom they couldn't see very often. My family is very close-knit. I was praying every single day, and still am today, for her to be in our life to know us, to know that she has another family and that we love her very much. I understand life and relationships are not always perfect.

After saying goodbye to my brother and parents at the airport, I met up with an old friend who used to live in Tiszadob and now worked as an airport police officer. She took Luke and me straight to the front of the queue for security.

We had a good flight and the steward helped to hold Luke while I got into my seat and fastened my seatbelt. Luke was such a good boy, and again he slept almost the entire flight.

I couldn't wait to see James again. He'd been working in Essex and timed his return to Bath to pick us up from Heathrow. It was always a special moment when we were reunited after time spent apart, and Luke was happy too.

Everything returned to normal. The next day I unpacked our bags and I continued working my way through the questions for my childcare NVQ course. Sometimes I thought that when my maternity leave finished I would take Luke with me to the nursery and it would all be easy for us. And I dreamed one day of having my own nursery, with international children.

CHAPTER SIX

Bad News, Very Bad News

*I wait for the Lord, my soul waits, and in his word I put my
hope. My soul waits for the Lord more than the watchmen wait
for the morning, more than the watchmen wait for the morning.*
Psalm 130:5,6

I started to notice that Luke was a little uncomfortable at times.
He woke up a lot in the night and now cried seemingly without
reason. He could only roll himself from his back on to one side,
not the other side. In addition, his head seemed to always be
positioned at an awkward angle; when he was sitting upright it was
lolling to one side.

He had recently started to scratch the back of his head and had
made it dry. I mentioned this to the health visitor but she wasn't
concerned about it and he had some skin cream prescribed for his
head. She suggested it might be eczema. To that I replied, "It's not
possible because his skin isn't dry on any other part of his body, and I
look after his skin very well." It's very common for babies to have
eczema but I couldn't believe that Luke had it.

I still wasn't happy and so I decided to take him to the doctor. I explained that I thought at his age he should be able to hold his head properly and roll over to both sides. The doctor replied that he was looking fine but gave us some other cream for his head and changed his body wash just in case.

Luke started to cry more often, including in his sleep, and it took him a long time to settle. Then one day he vomited after his morning milk and this carried on during the day. I decided to take him back to the doctor. This time she suggested it might be diarrhoea and sickness. I wasn't happy with that answer as I knew Luke managed his poo well and his behaviour had changed; he was less interested in things, spent time just looking at the wall and was also vomiting. So she sent me home with Dioralyte, an oral rehydration powder that you dissolve in water, and told me to just wait until he was settled and to make sure he didn't get dehydrated.

When a mother feels something isn't right, then it isn't right. The next day Luke was the same, so I asked for an urgent appointment at the GP and asked James to come with me and to be assertive that we wanted to go to the hospital for him to be checked over. This time we saw a different doctor and we told her everything from the beginning again. She understood our concern and phoned the children's ward at the hospital to let them know we would be taking him straight over there.

It took a very long time to wait for someone to see us. Then finally someone came to examine Luke; they thought it was a stomach bug and as he hadn't got any other symptoms they sent us home. They instructed us to carry on with the Dioralyte but to give it to him using a syringe, as he was refusing to drink from his bottle and by this time I didn't have enough milk so we were feeding him both breast milk and formula.

Back at home we tried using the syringe to give Luke the Dioralyte solution. We had to aim for 5ml every five minutes; however, it took most of five minutes to give him the 5ml because he didn't want to open his mouth. This made it a full time, nonstop job while he was awake. It was ridiculous.

The next day, Thursday, James had an important meeting in London and we agreed that he would go as long as Luke wasn't sick overnight, which he wasn't. His mum was coming to visit anyway so she would be around. He left early in the morning and I became more worried throughout the day. I decided, "That's it, I am going to go back to the hospital and we're not coming home until I know why Luke is sleepier than usual and why he's crying like he's in pain." James' mum arrived at the hospital and it was good for her to be on my side as I was concerned it really wasn't just a stomach infection.

The next day, after Luke and I had stayed the night in hospital, yet another doctor examined him and then measured his head circumference. She didn't say anything apart from asking when the last time was that it had been measured. I answered, "When he was six weeks old."

Later, the doctor came back with another doctor, who took one look at Luke's head and remarked, "It shouldn't be that big." So he decided to take an ultrasound scan of it. After the scan, the doctor informed us that Luke had more fluid in his brain than usual and that something might be pressing a nerve, stopping the fluid from draining. He wanted him to have an MRI scan.

I started to cry as I already began to imagine the worst, and I called James to come immediately from home, where he was working, to the hospital. I left Luke with James' mum and went to meet James as he arrived, to tell him face to face what we knew so far.

Back on the children's ward, they wanted to take blood but it was very difficult to find any veins. Luke cried a lot and I was upset that I couldn't calm him down the way I knew best.

James and I went with him to have the MRI scan. He had to lie down and be strapped on to a special bed that would move into the middle of the doughnut-shaped scanner. We could see his face through an angled mirror positioned above his head and he watched us from where he was. By that time, he wasn't upset anymore, even though the noise was really loud from the scanning machine. During the whole scan he just sucked on his dummy as we kept talking to him. Afterwards, I immediately gave Luke a big cuddle and we went back to our room on the ward to wait for the result.

It was now late in the day, well into the early evening. By that time my brother Matyi had arrived to be with me. The doctor came in with a nurse and told us that the scan showed there was a growth in his brain and that we would be sent immediately to Frenchay Hospital in Bristol, which was a hospital specialising in neurology until its later closure in 2014. They told us he needed an operation to relieve the pressure in his brain that evening.

I had no idea what the doctor was talking about and what was happening, but I understood that it was a big deal. We waited for the ambulance to arrive and I went with Luke. James drove home quickly to get more clothes and essentials, and then drove to Bristol – again quickly – with his mum and my brother. I told my brother to phone my parents to let them know what was going on and keep them informed.

That night, everything started to collapse around us.

When we arrived at Frenchay Hospital, about half an hour later, we were put in one of two rooms in the High Dependency Unit of the children's ward. As we waited for James and the others to arrive, a nurse explained what the monitor was showing – Luke's heart rate, breathing rate and oxygen saturations – so we could check the levels too, although of course it would sound an alarm if the numbers went above or below the parameters. James and his mum and my brother arrived shortly after. One of the neurosurgeons came and explained the scan pictures and told us that Luke had a tumour in the back of his head, in the cerebellum. Then I realised why he had been scratching the back of his head for the past few weeks; he had been in discomfort.

The neurosurgeon explained that they needed to make a careful plan to remove the tumour and because it was a weekend they would not perform such a big operation yet as they would have to get the right team together. We asked about the operation to relieve the pressure that the doctor in Bath had told us about. However, the neurosurgeon replied, "It's best not to do operations during the night because that's when mistakes get made." Instead they would perform this less serious operation the next morning. Unfortunately, with Luke's condition deteriorating – he kept vomiting and his heart rate gradually decreased – a few hours later that is exactly what they decided to do; they would operate during the night. They urgently needed to drain some brain fluid[13] to reduce the pressure in his brain and this would make him feel a bit better.

---

[13] Cerebral Spinal Fluid or CSF

A little earlier in the evening, before we had known they would operate during the night, James' mum had asked us in tears if we wanted to get Luke christened in case anything happened. We felt very confused and didn't want to even contemplate losing him. She went off to phone Patrick, the rector from church, to come and see us the next morning before we expected the operation to take place. Then a little later she left the hospital and went to stay the night at a friend's house who happened to live nearby.

I phoned my mum and asked if she could come. "Of course," she agreed. We just needed to book a flight for her. However, there was no Wi-Fi and hardly any mobile signal, so James called Haze, his sister, to ask her help in booking the flight. She found a flight from Budapest to London Luton for early the next morning. I quickly called Mum back and she said this would be fine; Dad could take her to the airport. James phoned his dad, who by this time had decided to come to the hospital the next day anyway, to ask if he could pick her up from Luton on his way, to which he agreed. We then had to worry about whether they would recognise each other and be able to communicate, as my mum couldn't speak any English and nor could James' dad speak Hungarian.

A little later on, another doctor came to find Luke's vein again to insert a cannula. Everything turned into a nightmare. Nurses came to make observations every hour and they got him ready for theatre. We went with him to the anaesthetic room and took his favourite soft toy, Mr Snail, and pulled the string to play the soothing music while he fell into the anaesthetic sleep. I kissed his forehead and said, "God bless you!" and told him how much I loved him and that we would see him soon.

We had to go back to Luke's room to wait for him. There the nurses offered us tea and toast, which we accepted. James ate and drank but I felt nauseous and couldn't eat anything.

Luke spent three-and-a-half hours in the theatre. While he was there, questions started to fill my mind – How could this happen? Why us? Why him? – and I pleaded with God to help me, to help my son. "Please look after him."

We tried to get a bit of sleep. Then, in the very early hours of the morning, at about two o'clock, they brought Luke back to the room. They had performed a procedure called a "third ventriculostomy" to help the fluid drain in his brain, and had inserted an ommaya reservoir so that fluid could be drained again without going to theatre. They had connected a tube to the ommaya reservoir to drain the fluid and we had to make sure his head was always above the drain so that any excess fluid could drain out with gravity.

Luke was sleepy but when I got into the cot with him, he could feel my presence. That night I didn't care about anything except to be with him and I lay with him in that tiny cot. I held his hand and started to pray: "Lord, help me to trust your plan, even when I don't understand it. I am in great pain. Help me to hold on through the darkness and wait for the light to dawn. Amen."

This prayer has stayed firmly imprinted on my mind to this day.

The night after the operation, Luke slept quite well. Our rector, Patrick, turned up early Saturday morning. We decided not to christen Luke but instead Patrick prayed for him and for us. We kept in touch and, naturally, we wanted Patrick to ask everyone in church to pray for him too.

A little later on in the morning, the doctors came by on their ward round and the surgeon showed us the MRI scan pictures. He explained again that Luke had a tumour at the back of his head – a type called an ependymoma. They described it as "very aggressive" and "extremely rare in children"; in fact, only around two hundred children a year are diagnosed with any kind of brain tumour in the UK and about ten percent of these are ependymomas. It most commonly affects children under five years of age. They told us that the location of the tumour could affect his breathing and swallowing, and it was about the size of a golf ball. They had to remove it but while he was still stable and didn't have a build-up of pressure in his brain, the team had to get together to plan the big operation.

We asked how risky the operation was and how long it would take. They explained it would be very long and there was no guarantee that they could remove all of the tumour, but of course they would try their best. It would only be in the theatre when they found it that they could see how differentiated it looked from the healthy brain tissue and therefore how much damage they could avoid. There was a risk of causing "temporary or permanent neurological deficit" and a risk of death. They were planning this operation for the following Friday.

We were in tears for days and couldn't stop wondering how it could have happened. I felt I needed my parents so much and later in the morning Mum arrived with James' dad. It was so good to have her by my side and I felt my own dad's support as well from a distance. It was difficult to look after myself; I hardly ate anything.

When Luke felt a bit better and my brother was entertaining him by making him smile with funny faces and sounds, I managed to eat and drink a bit. I settled down on the cot to feed him. I didn't know it then but this would be the last time I would breastfeed him. He was so settled when he was with me, but then he started to repeatedly vomit and could hardly turn his neck.

The next day was Sunday. We went to the Hospital Chapel for the Sunday Service, where there was just a handful of other people. In the evening we moved our belongings into one of the parents' rooms upstairs where we were able to stay.

Over the next day or two, Luke's heart rate again began to decline, and the medical staff decided they needed to get on and do the debulking[14] as an emergency operation. So much for the detailed planning and assembling the right team... They said they couldn't wait for the specialist equipment that would monitor if they were causing any damage to Luke's brain; they just had to get on and do it in order to save his life again.

So our days darkened.

Before the operation we went into a Quiet Room and had a chat with the team. They informed us that Luke was not very well. The drain that they had inserted was working but it was causing the tumour to be pulled up through the brain, which wasn't good. They needed to remove the tumour even sooner than planned. They warned us that it was very risky and he might not pull through.

My world collapsed – I didn't want to hear this.

We had to sign the consent form but of course we trusted them with all our heart and just wanted Luke to get better. It was the early evening by the time we walked through the corridors with him being wheeled in the cot down to the anaesthetic room, bringing Mr Snail with us again. I kissed him as never before, with tears on my face,

---

[14] removal of the tumour

and said, "Love you and see you soon." My final words were, "God bless you."

They couldn't tell us how long the operation would be, except to say it would be "very long". They promised to keep us updated and let us know what was happening from time to time. They took us to a Quiet Room in the Intensive Care Unit, and Mum and Matyi stayed there with us too. It had a bathroom and kitchen facilities, so we kept making cups of tea and ate some sandwiches that they brought us. We sat, mostly in silence, for hour after hour after hour. Waiting, hoping, praying. Eventually, at around two o'clock in the morning, someone knocked on the door and came in with the news that the operation was nearly finished.

A little while later a nurse came to take us to see Luke. She took us into the Paediatric Acute Care Unit (PACU), which was just a room off from the main Intensive Care Unit, and warned us that he was on ventilation and there were lots of tubes.

It was a great shock to see him connected to so many machines and painful to see him with a big bandage on his head and with machines, tubes and catheters all around him, and various medicines being pumped into him. One of the nurses explained that they had to keep him asleep and sedated. Shortly after, the surgeon came and said Luke had managed well during the operation and hadn't needed any blood transfusions. They had removed some of the tumour and had kept the drain in his head. They still had to make a plan for the bigger operation; this one had just been a rushed emergency operation in which they had removed what they could without risking too much damage.

The nurse told us they would be monitoring him very closely, never leaving him alone, so we shouldn't be worried. It was so hard to deal with all the new medical information at once and we continually had lots of questions. "What is this for?" "What is that for?" Of course we wanted to know everything.

I kissed Luke straightaway and held his hand. Although he was heavily sedated, he started to move his arm in a strange way – repetitively and with a twitch. We wondered if he was having a fit and one of the doctors came over immediately and confirmed it. Luke needed to have a CT scan to see if everything was alright. To get to the scan, however, he had to be disconnected from the ventilator so the anaesthetist used the bag and oxygen to control his breathing. When we got the results back they informed us that he had had a stroke and there was a blood clot built up that needed to be removed as an emergency in the morning, just a few hours away.

I couldn't believe that within just twenty-four hours, Luke was having two major emergency neuro-operations. We went with him again to the anaesthetic room and I said, "God bless you, baby, and see you soon." Once again we were informed it would be a long operation. This time, however, just the two of us waited together; we no longer wanted to see and talk to other people, family or otherwise.

We were given the Quiet Room on the ward to wait in, but this time we did not stay there for the whole period. Instead we went to the chapel. It was so peaceful and quiet. I started to pray very earnestly. "Oh God, tell me what is happening with us. We were so happy and wanted Luke so much in our life. Please show me what I have done wrong. What do I need to do to make it better? Hold Luke and don't take him away."

I couldn't stop thinking about this. When he had been a newborn baby I had thanked God so much that our little boy was in our life, and healthy. We were so happy that everything seemed perfect. But it can't always be that way! Life is not perfect and everyone experiences a difficult journey of some sort. I didn't want to reject God because I needed him so much, but on the other hand I asked why he had let this happen to us. Surely God is good, so he has to be good with everyone? We went back and forth between the room and the chapel, and the nurses brought us sandwiches and snacks. At last, one of the nurses from PACU came to tell us that Luke was back. Once again it had turned into a really long day; this operation had been the same length as the previous one: eight hours.

Fortunately, Luke hadn't needed a blood transfusion this time either. They had removed some more of the tumour; there was still some left but the good news was they thought they could take it all out next time. We started to read to him and I spoke into his ear, telling him how proud I was and that he was doing so well. I said sorry to him that things had gone wrong and told him that he did not deserve all this. It was so hard to see him lying on the bed as he did. He was just a little boy who needed fun, playtime and cuddling time, but he lay there asleep all day and all night.

I watched the nurse feeding Luke with a syringe through the NG[15] tube and she asked me how he was fed at home. I said that he was mainly breastfed and I suddenly realised it had been a few days since I had last given him milk. "I've still got some," I said, so she suggested that I should try to express some milk to add to the special medical milk given to him. I cried. I didn't want Luke to lose this special connection with me but I didn't have a breast pump and there weren't any at the hospital. However, they requested one from the larger hospital on the other side of the city and it was delivered by taxi. My milk wasn't enough, of course, and he needed all the nutrition he could get to keep him going, but it felt good that at least he was having something from me.

The nurses always let us knew how Luke had been during the night and whether there were any changes. Because he had been in PACU for a few days by now, one of them also invited us to help with his care – mainly washing his face and nappy area. The latter wasn't particularly dirty since he had a catheter inserted and hadn't had much milk. We couldn't say no! We wanted him to feel and know that we were there with him, as his eyes were still closed the whole time. When we washed him we talked to him and I sang all the songs we had sung at home just like normal.

Luke had physio sessions every day, which was mainly to work on clearing out secretions from his chest, since he was still on ventilation. This was very difficult to watch at first as it looked really rough and as if it was hurting him – the physiotherapist pushed his chest down hard and repeated rapidly – but of course we knew he had to have it done. They also taught us gentle exercises to move his arms and legs, and we learned how to move him every hour to avoid bed sores and reduce the swelling; firstly, he'd be lying on his left, then his back, then his right.

We received many phone calls and text messages from friends and family but couldn't concentrate on updating everyone, only our closest family and friends. Our church were giving us a lot of support and my lovely friend Mandy came to visit us and passed on updates to others at church. She brought food for us, which was so kind. Back in the summer, Luke and I had spent a lovely sunny day in her garden

---

[15] nasogastric

and had a good conversation about our faith. I kept thinking back to her words when I was confused about God. She had said that God never leaves us, that we are much loved by him and that he was looking after Luke. I realised that God had used people around me so that I could get to know him more. He knew I still needed him.

We had a meeting with the neurosurgeon and met an oncology consultant and specialist oncology nurse about starting chemotherapy for Luke. Because it was an aggressive brain tumour, they had to treat it as soon as he was well enough to handle the chemotherapy. I didn't know much – hardly anything, really – about cancer and treatment. I had heard about some treatments but didn't know which could be used for different kinds of cancers. At first we didn't know why he needed chemotherapy if the surgeons could surgically remove all of the tumour. They explained to us that even if the tumour growth was all removed as far as they could see, there could still be microscopic cancer cells flowing within the CSF around the brain and spine, and it was important to kill these cells to stop the cancer coming back.

I knew a bit about chemotherapy. I knew it was risky too and had many side effects, and that it could be long term. I felt that by agreeing to this, we were going to be poisoning him. But we had no choice, really.

Surgical removal of the tumour is the first and most important stage in treatment. So far, Luke had had three operations, two of which were emergency debulk operations to remove some of the tumour, but not carried out in a fully planned manner with the ideal team. The neurosurgeon told us one further planned operation was required to remove the remaining tumour. He explained it was a very risky operation and what the risks were – again, a 5-10% chance of death during the operation – and what the expected outcome was. This would be the longest operation so far, he said. But we signed the consent form and knew Luke was receiving the best possible treatment; the surgeon had done well so far, so we trusted him. This operation would be on Thursday, and Luke would be first on the list.

On Thursday morning, when the time came to take Luke down to theatre, we said our goodbyes. We went down to the theatre with him together and I took a card that my mother-in-law had given me from the hospital chapel and put it next to him. It read, "When I sit in darkness the Lord will be a light to me."[16]

I kissed Luke's forehead and his lips, and told him, "I will wait for you here and I will see you again, my baby. God will be with you." Every time he went to sleep under general anaesthetic I broke into tears. It was so hard to maintain my strength whilst wondering if the day that had passed would be my last with him. I was very afraid of death and that fear grew each day.

This time, as we knew that this would be an all-day operation, we had to choose between waiting the whole time doing nothing or trying to take our mind off things. So this time we went back up to our room and James got stuck into his church finance work – he had a lot of catching up to do, making payments and logging receipts and payments in the accounting software – and tried not to think too much about what Luke was going through. I was amazed how he was able to clear his mind from what was going on.

I just didn't know what to do. I decided to take my childcare coursework and do some writing during this operation.

On several occasions, James and I went out. We held each other's hands tightly and went to the chapel, lit candles and prayed. My prayer was, "Please forgive me if I have done anything wrong. I don't know why this is happening to Luke, to us, but show me that you are a really great God. I trust you. Please heal him and put your hand on Luke's brain and take the whole tumour out, and put your other hand on his heart and keep him alive. Give energy to the doctors, the team, and make sure that everything goes well, in Jesus' name. Amen."

Those were the longest hours I have ever spent without my baby. How could I pass the day? I was just waiting for them to phone us. But they didn't. The whole day passed with no news. James and I ate a little lunch, then we went back to our room and he read the Bible. I started to read too and randomly opened at the book of Luke. In fact, I read the whole of Luke's Gospel. We kept going back to the chapel, then sometimes to the Quiet Room, had a coffee, then James continued doing his church work and I lay in bed and imagined God's hand on Luke's head and heart.

---

[16] Micah 7:8

As the day turned into evening, I fell asleep, as did James. We had hardly slept when at about eleven o'clock in the evening we received the phone call to say that Luke was out from the theatre and we could go and see him. We ran all the way down to PACU and couldn't wait for them to buzz us in. Then I saw my tiny baby – and of course he was sleeping. They needed to keep him sedated because he was still on ventilation, and had lots of strong medicines to keep his pain under control. Approaching midnight, the neurosurgeon arrived and said the operation had gone well and he thought the whole tumour had been removed, but they would check with an MRI scan the next day. He was pleased with how the operation had gone and Luke had done amazingly well; he hadn't needed a blood transfusion this time either. The neurosurgeon admitted that he might have damaged some nerves, and maybe vision through Luke's right eye would be blurred or he might not be able to see through it at all; also, he didn't think Luke would be able to hear with the right ear. Physically he would be a bit weak on the right side generally. We didn't care too much about these things; we were just glad that he was alive and back from theatre after such a mammoth operation – thirteen hours. During this long, long operation, he had been lying face down on his front for the whole time and the pressure had caused a lot of swelling in his face. In addition, he had one large red pressure sore right across his forehead.

The nurses sent us to sleep and said not to be worried as they were looking after Luke and we needed to get some rest. So we went to bed and I started to cry in my prayer. I thanked God that he was with my son and that he heard my prayers.

The next day we went to see Luke and the nurse asked me if I wanted to hold and cuddle him. I cried again. "Is that really possible? I haven't been able to have cuddles for days." I had desperately wanted to hold him and now I could. They were very careful when lifting him from the bed with the many tubes and cables on his body. They put him on a pillow on my lap and I just watched him, kissed him, and told him how much I loved him. We had some visits from close family and friends. It was good to have Mum around. Sometimes we didn't talk with each other but it was enough just to feel she was there.

I kept expressing my milk, which kept me going, and it was fed to Luke through the tube. Then they took the bandage off and I could stroke his head for the first time. The doctors wanted to wake him up gradually and he opened his eyes. I didn't know if he could see me much but I kept talking to him. Sometimes he gripped my hand or moved his legs a bit. All these little things were overwhelming.

The doctors told us that he needed to be transferred to Bristol Children's Hospital now that all his neurosurgery was complete, because they didn't have much room at Frenchay – only two paediatric intensive care bed spaces – and he would need to be at the Children's Hospital to recover. It was sad and disruptive leaving this amazing team that we had got used to, but we greatly thanked them for how they had looked after our little boy.

Chapter Seven

Getting Used to our New Life

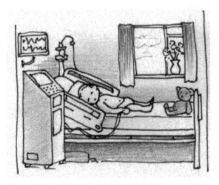

I travelled in the ambulance with Luke down to the Children's Hospital, and James drove our car crammed full of all our bags and Haze and Matyi, who were visiting us at the time. This time I couldn't sit with Luke because there were already too many people in the back of the ambulance looking after him, so I was seated in the front of the vehicle. I saw how the ambulance drives through traffic as the traffic was very heavy even on such a short journey. When we arrived, James and I couldn't see Luke straightaway as they had to get him settled in his cot; instead we had to wait in the parents' kitchen, a small room which was very busy with other children's relatives. After a short while they called us to see him.

I had thought Luke would have his own room but instead he was put in a very large intensive care room. There were twenty beds around both sides of a large open space with the nurses' station in the middle. I could see lots of other ill children close up and this was rather frightening; there were many machines and monitors beeping continuously and some children on ventilation. It was busy and noisy, but of course I tried to concentrate just on Luke. Some doctors came around and introduced themselves to us. They explained that we would see many different doctors because the hospital was large. This turned out to be precisely the case.

Soon afterwards we became very busy. Luke's oncologist and oncology specialist nurse whom we'd met the previous week came down to see how we were doing and how Luke was settling in. We talked more about when the chemotherapy would start; they said they wanted to start as soon as he was doing better. We signed the consent form. They told us he needed a quick operation to insert a Hickman line which would be used for taking blood and giving chemotherapy. It's a type of central line that is inserted in the chest and the line goes into a major vein, so the nurse wouldn't need to use a needle every time for taking blood or a cannula for giving intravenous medicines. Over time we found out just how essential it was. They taught how to keep the skin, line and dressing clean and healthy.

Luke was quite poorly and he was still on lots of strong medications such as morphine, but they tried to wean him off slowly. Every day he made small steps of progress, such as moving his hands and legs a little bit, and opening his eyes, but they needed to maintain a background level of sedation due to him still being on ventilation, so if he appeared to be moving "too much" the nurses would just give him more medicine. We started to be concerned about his level of sedation and felt they were giving him too many medicines unnecessarily.

A few of the nurses were particularly pleasant and had great communication skills, automatically telling us what medicines they were giving Luke and what was planned for the day ahead, but not all of them did. We asked one of the doctors for a list of medicines that he was having and how often, so we could follow it, and ended up with a list down one side of A4 paper of about twenty-five different medicines. He had a physiotherapy session every day and we had more opportunities to cuddle; these sessions were very difficult but worth it of course.

Because Luke was doing well, they wanted to take him off the ventilation, so they began weaning the oxygen levels down to normal air and reducing the pressure so he could begin to do more work in managing his own breathing. He was on the ventilation machine for five weeks, which is quite a long time, and we hoped he would be able to get back to normal breathing on his own.

By this time James had started to go back to work, so most of the time during the day I was on my own and there were restrictions on when I could visit Luke, such as not during the morning ward round from eight until ten. After a few days of sleeping in the parents' accommodation in the hospital we were fortunate enough to get a room at the Ronald McDonald House. This is a large house, usually available for parents of children in intensive care, and we could stay there for as long as necessary. We found this really useful because there was a large kitchen in which we could cook, rather than just eating microwave food, and we had an en suite. The house wasn't far from the hospital so we could walk there; it took about ten minutes to get up to where Luke was.

I was quite excited on the day they tried to take him off the ventilator completely. It was such a big step and it felt strange that James wasn't with me. Luke came out of theatre, where they had extubated[17] him, inside an oxygen tent, and he tried to move as though he wanted to talk to me. However, a few hours later he started to struggle and they had to re-intubate him. This time the tube was fed through his mouth not through his nose as it had been before.

A few days later they tried again to extubate him, but after a few hours, he became exhausted and struggled with his breathing. This was so hard to watch. The nurse looking after him that night didn't seem to care much about him. Unlike the other nurses, she didn't speak to us or explain what she was doing as she went about looking after him. He developed a sternal recession, which is where, as he attempted to breath in, the middle of his chest dipped really, really low. We were very concerned but she didn't seem worried. When we kept repeating that he was in serious difficulty, she finally said she could give him some paracetamol to help. We were very upset and

---

[17] removal of the ventilation tube

told her he didn't need paracetamol, he needed oxygen. We had an argument and called the doctor to sort Luke out immediately with some medicines to help him breath. This turned out to be one of several issues we ended up having with this particular nurse.

We were so disappointed as we had thought Luke was in the best care, yet we had no confidence in the nurse looking after him on this particular nightshift. So we decided we would stay with him all through the night to make sure he was OK. James stayed by Luke's side until 3am while I slept in our room, and then we swapped. The next day James had a word with the ward sister to tell her what had happened and that we didn't want that nurse looking after Luke again. The sister apologised and said it was surprising as she was an experienced nurse-trainer.

Luke was re-intubated and put back on ventilation once again. This was a disappointing backwards step but at least we knew his breathing was safe. As he had been on ventilation for such a long time, the ENT[18] team came to check on him and they said that because he hadn't managed to breathe on his own successfully, he needed a tracheostomy to breathe through. This was not familiar to us so we asked many questions. They explained the surgical procedure and that the tracheostomy would be easier to breathe through as it's a shorter airway and doesn't involve the larynx[19].

Again, we had to give our consent to this, but I was concerned about how we would cope with it as it would require a lot of care and attention for an extended period. Luke had to go to theatre for the operation; I kissed him in my usual way and we just waited. This time it didn't take too long and it was good to see his face without the breathing tube and lots of tape holding it in place, but of course it was equally strange to see the tube going into his throat. The nurses needed to suction him very frequently.

They explained to us about changing the tracheostomy dressing every day; how to suction him, which is about removing anything he has coughed up, secretions from the chest or any mis-swallowed saliva; and changing the tube every week. They told us that we needed to learn to do all these things as quickly as possible. My first thought was that I didn't think I could; I was so worried that I would

---

[18] Ear, Nose and Throat
[19] voice box

make a mistake and cause harm. But when James started to do his first suction, it made me realise that I could do it too. It was important for Luke to feel that we, his parents, were there, and we were much more gentle with him as we were caring for our own son; the nurses were just doing their job.

We were there when they changed the tube the first time, and we could see the stoma – the hole in Luke's throat – for the first time. It was hard for me to watch and think that I would need to be doing this myself very soon. Little could I have imagined that in a few months' time I would be teaching nurses and student nurses how to do the same thing. Back then we used to call a nurse every few minutes to suction Luke; now it's completely normal.

Luke felt much better and it was a relief that he didn't need to be on ventilation; his whole body swelling started to get better. He began to watch us more and be more interested in his environment. He followed the light with his eyes so we put a coloured light tube around the cot and he started to reach for it and hold it in his tiny hand.

Because I hadn't been able to feed him, and by this time I couldn't express any more milk, I wanted him to really feel I was close to him. I started to put a dummy in his mouth just to remind him. He had used a dummy from when he was seven weeks old but had not been able to use one over the previous month or so. At first he didn't have the muscle control to be able to hold the dummy in his mouth or suck it; but before long he got the hang of it again. When he was unsettled I would climb into his cot with him and everyone was surprised that I was tiny enough to fit there. I didn't see anything wrong in doing that; I just felt we had to be close as he was still my baby.

A speech and language therapist came to help us with the right side of his face which had a palsy, and to teach him how to eat again and how to swallow. They were happy that I had started to give Luke his dummy to help the muscles to move. I felt it was natural; I knew what my son needed. I stroked his face as well to stimulate the nerves. Then we noticed he started to be a bit sleepier and his ommaya reservoir started to grow, a growing lump on his head. The doctors said he was fine but because we had been with him all the time we recognised this as a change. We asked them to check and he was given a scan which showed he was suffering from Hydrocephalus, a build-up of fluid in the brain. They had to tap his ommaya reservoir to reduce the pressure once again, and the neurosurgeons decided he needed a ventriculoperitoneal shunt which would be inserted into his brain to drain excess fluid down to his abdomen. This operation was carried out on December 1st, but because it was neurosurgery, it took place at Frenchay Hospital. We weren't allowed to go with him so it was very strange waiting back at the Children's Hospital whilst Luke underwent surgery at a different hospital.

I found myself asking, "Why does he have to go through all this again?" I pleaded with God, "Please, no more trouble again because I don't know how I can cope with anything more."

The doctors said it would be a quick and easy operation and he would feel better, and indeed within a couple of hours he was back. They said he had been looking around in the ambulance and enjoyed the ride. They explained that for a few days he would need to be kept tilted at an angle to encourage the fluid to drain from his brain with gravity, and not to lie on his left side. Because we didn't know how much he could see and the nerves didn't work on that side, they decided Luke needed a lubricating ointment applied every four hours or so. So much to remember... James and I decided to write daily notes from this point onward as a point of reference for us to remember what we'd been told and as a kind of diary of how Luke was, so we could give him the best care possible. Around this time the doctors started to wean him off lots of strong medications like steroids, which was a positive sign.

We had a big meeting to plan Luke's discharge. Of course it was still a long time off but we needed to start to organise how we would be looked after once we got home. I felt very worried and was not confident to go home in January and take over everything. He needed so much care and I didn't feel it was a one-person job. But they mentioned a place called Charlton Farm Children's Hospice where we could have respite breaks, with carers who could look after Luke while we were away or just be around. We also had a discussion about respite at home if we needed.

Luke stopped needing hourly observations; these decreased to four-hourly which was an encouraging sign that he was on the mend.

Although he was no longer on ventilation, he was on humidified air. A tube still loosely attached with tapes around his neck provided warm, humidified air to the tracheostomy, which meant that, with all the other cables and lines, he wasn't very free to be able to be moved around.

There was a little child with chicken pox on the intensive care ward and because Luke had started his chemotherapy, he went into a side room. Meanwhile, we waited for a bed on the oncology ward. James' sister Haze came to visit us and we gave cuddles to Luke. Then something amazing happened; after two months without smiling he smiled at me, although only with the left side of his face – and it was wonderful to share this experience with Haze, as James was at work. Haze took some pictures. I made funny noises and played peekaboo through my tears of joy – and he kept smiling.

Haze could see on my face how much I had waited for this moment to arrive and we cried together. Luke had a nap and while he slept we went out for lunch together and called James at work to let him know the exciting news.

On the way out from the ward we bumped into the neurosurgeon who had carried out most of Luke's operations and he answered some questions we had. Haze desperately wanted to know if Luke could attend school later on and whether he would be 'normal' like other children. He told us that Luke's brain would continue to develop as well as his body. He might stay a bit weaker on his right side, as well as with reduced hearing and vision on the right, but, yes, he would be able to attend normal school and live a normal life. He mentioned that we could try to take out the tracheostomy after a year; he didn't think he would need it for any longer. At last we had received some good news about Luke's future. It was our most positive day so far.

Luke become nauseous and starting vomiting because of the chemotherapy. The chemotherapy protocol meant he had one dose every two weeks, and there were four different combinations of different chemotherapy agents, as the complete cycle lasted eight weeks. So we really had to be aware of which one he was getting and when. The chemotherapy was administered intravenously into his Hickman line over a period of twenty-four, forty-eight or seventy-two hours depending on which chemicals were being given. He had blood taken every day to check the counts of his red and white blood cells, and check he was well enough for the next dose.

Since he had been in hospital, he was on a special medical dietary milk and because he was vomiting so much during the chemotherapy days, the nurses decided to slow down his food rate and then build it up from there. This meant at times he was only getting 10ml of milk per hour, or 240ml per day – hardly anything. A few times, because he was sick so often, the doctors decided to stop his milk altogether and just give intravenous fluids.

Luke was slowly weaned off the humidified air and used a 'Swedish nose' heat and moisture exchanger, a small filter attachment on the end of his tracheostomy tube.

Finally, there was space for us to move to the oncology ward. The staff there had been briefed about Luke and all the nurses were excited to meet him. They gave their best; they were all very helpful and made us feel comfortable on the ward. Luke had his own room and we started to decorate it for him. We met a play specialist called Jeanette and she asked me what he liked. I could hardly say anything; I had only just started to get to know him myself. But I answered that he liked light and mobiles that hang from the ceiling.

Luke had no tubes or cables attached to him anymore, other than for feeding, so I was able to pick him up anytime that I wanted to cuddle him or change his position. I did this very slowly and carefully as his head was still sensitive. He had physiotherapy every day and we had some floor time, and he got a foam chair as well to sit on and encourage him to be a bit more mobile. This became a fun time for both of us. There was Wi-Fi so we could video call my parents in Hungary and we had visitors a few times every week. Mama Pam came to visit us regularly and Grandad Martin and Jenny took me out for lunch when Luke had naps. (James was at work.) My brother came most Saturdays or Sundays. It was nice to have visitors and for Luke to get to know his family. I spent most of the time in his cot, which they found funny on the ward, but I said I had got used to it and it was easier then standing the whole day next to him. Luke's mattress changed from a special temperature-controlled one, used in intensive care to help regulate his temperature, to a normal hospital cot mattress. He had his ups and downs. Sometimes we had to deal with high temperatures or infections, high blood pressure or high heart rate; in fact, almost everything that you can imagine in a hospital.

Christmastime came and we tried to do our best to make Luke's first Christmas an enjoyable and memorable one. He received so many presents. We had a big Christmas meal provided for all the staff, parents and patients which we ate in the corridor of the ward, with Christmas music playing. I thanked God that we could celebrate our Christmas together and also that James and I had found a youthful church near our accommodation where we could go when we were able to.

I felt God giving me strength every day and believed that he knew I could manage. I remembered praying around the time of Luke's birth, thanking God that he was healthy – and now I was thanking him that he was still with me.

After having been in hospital for a few months, one evening, when Luke had gone to sleep, James and I left the hospital for a few hours. We went to James' friend Stu's house where they were having a dinner with their friends. It felt strange to be away from our son and we tried not to worry about him too much, but it was difficult.

Luke had an ENT review. We found out his right vocal cord was paralysed, which they said meant he might not be able to shout or talk loudly in the future. In fact, he couldn't talk or make any sounds at all but we could see when he was happy and his face laughed without making a sound. Whenever I would tell friends that Luke was happy and laughing, they would ask me what he sounded like. I had to explain that he made no sound but that it was amazing to see his face.

He had a lot of fun as we wanted to make his life as happy and easy as possible. He started to become a big fan of balloons and balls. We had very many balloons in the room.

He also had his first bath for many months, which wasn't easy as he had a Hickman line and dressing which we needed to keep absolutely dry, tracheostomy tube, dressing and tapes around his neck to keep dry, and the NG tube dangling down his back. We needed to cover them over but Luke didn't like the water and he didn't like anything that touched his skin. So it wasn't a difficult decision to go back to bed-bathing him from then on.

Then the day came when I did my first tracheostomy tube change. I was so proud of it! Luke felt comfortable and I was very calm during the change, as was he. I realized there was nothing to worry about at all for him and that he was happy. I just chatted to him during the change. I wasn't at all frightened to see the stoma, the hole in his neck. James and I did a short first aid course as well at the hospital to ensure we were prepared for any eventuality.

We had a follow-up discharge meeting about leaving the hospital soon, to go to our local hospital in Bath, before then making the move home. They talked about the team in Bath and while we were on this ward the team often came and introduced themselves so they wouldn't be strangers when we met them there. They also mentioned that we would needs lots of equipment and supplies for Luke's needs, including a special cot like in the hospital so he could lie at a good height for his tracheostomy care: daily dressing and tape changes, and weekly tube changes, as well as suctioning when he was asleep. We would have suction catheters, gloves, dressings, syringes, feed bottles and feed delivered to us, like a mini hospital.

James and I had a chat and decided that the place where we were living was not suitable for Luke and so we would need to find a new home. We didn't want to be far from the hospital and we also didn't want to have any stairs – and we needed plenty of space for everything.

James found a few places online and went back to Bath to look at them, as I was with Luke in the hospital the whole time, and eventually chose the fifth property. A few weeks later James moved without me being there, with the help of my brother and a few friends.

We met two CLIC Sargent nurses, Ally and Sarah, who would be involved with Luke when we returned home, helping by taking blood weekly to check his counts and giving any oncology care. We also met the nurses from the children's community team who would provide Luke's tracheostomy equipment and supplies. They explained that when we were home we would need a portable suction machine and have to take it everywhere we went, as well as an 'emergency bag' with us containing all we needed, such as spare tracheostomy tubes in case it accidentally came out or got blocked, or in case we needed to perform any emergency procedures. We also needed to take his emergency Hickman line kit around with us in case it broke or needed the end part replacing. They talked about oxygen as well but we didn't want to carry it around everywhere as Luke didn't need oxygen for most of the time, but we would have some at home in case.

While Luke was in hospital he had regular speech and language therapy, he had some purée to see how much he could swallow, if any, then he had a video fluoroscopy – lots of X-ray images taken in quick succession like a video, and using food with barium additive to show up on the X-ray – to see where the food went when it was swallowed. Because his right side didn't work properly we saw he needed more time to swallow the purée but sometimes it went down the wrong way and sometimes it was successfully swallowed down into his stomach. So from then on I tried to give him some purée whenever he was feeling well and not suffering too much from sickness.

They also showed us a speaking valve which could help Luke to use his voice. It was a one-way valve which allowed him to breathe in through the tracheostomy tube but exhale through his mouth and nose, meaning the air would pass through the larynx enabling him to make a sound. We tried to put it on and I heard a faint noise; it was unfamiliar but it was indeed Luke's voice. He couldn't cope with using it for long – only a few seconds at a time – so we didn't force it but we kept trying every day. He had fewer secretions and needed less suctioning, and we knew when to use the suction to clear them out; it all become normal for us.

We met a Hungarian doctor called Daniel. He worked on the oncology ward where we had been for a few weeks and it felt good to speak in my native tongue and fully understand all the medical words which I had heard every day. Because he was from Hungary, it made a difference to me. He examined Luke a few times during his stay, just to check him over or when we had any concerns about something, such as on a few of the occasions when spots appeared on his skin.

When Luke's blood results were poor, he needed to receive blood products: a blood transfusion of red blood cells when his haemoglobin was low, GCSF when his neutrophils were low and platelets when these were low.

Neurologically he was developing well and he was stronger day by day and quite happy. We met many families on the ward and I could mention one little girl in particular called Leah who was in the room next to Luke's. Her mum Jo and I met in the parents' kitchen and kept each other updated about our children. Leah had a brain tumour as well but hers was of a different type to Luke's. Leah was a lovely, smiley little girl around a year older than Luke and every time he and I passed their door, he always turned his head and smiled at her.

Luke started to turn in the bed on to each side – an amazing development. He reached for things when he needed them and clapped when he achieved something or got something that he wanted. It felt so good to see how he was starting to communicate with us. He loved looking at himself in the mirror and listening to music. I sang every day to him and performed actions with the songs too.

On one occasion the play therapist switched on the TV and there was a CBeebies program called Something Special, with Mr. Tumble, who uses Makaton sign language for children; he is really funny and educational as he talks and signs at the same time. I knew a little Makaton signing from nursery and started to do more with Luke.

On February 7th we said our goodbyes on the ward and were transferred to our local hospital (RUH) in Bath. After three months at the Children's Hospital we were happy to leave the ward and be closer to home. The CLIC nurse Sarah, our new doctor in Bath and some nurses came with a present for Luke.

It was such an emotional moment when I could finally say that we were 'home'. We discussed what was going to be provided by the Bath team and what Luke would need to go to Bristol Children's Hospital for – MRI scans and one particular chemotherapy drug. By this time James and I were confident with his care. We just told the nurses what we needed in his room to avoid continually asking them. We also explained our routine and care times, what we were doing and when.

We met other specialists like the physiotherapist and speech and language therapists who would take over these areas from Bristol to continue working with Luke in Bath. We scheduled appointments, and life became rather busy again.

Being at home would be another big change for us all. My mum gave up her job to come over to the UK and help us as we needed a second person for when James was out at work. She moved in with us

– this was the only workable solution. She learned how and what we did for Luke's care. I couldn't imagine being on my own with him at home when he was being sick and needed to have a suction to clear his airway as well as someone to hold him in the right position, as he couldn't sit up by himself yet, not to mention having to change the dressing when it got soaked in vomit – this is unquestionably a two-person job.

Mum learned everything really quickly and Luke felt very comfortable with her. That was a great relief as I could leave the ward for a while or have a coffee by myself. While Mum was with him I popped over to our new home to see it for the first time, as up until then only James had been there for the viewing and moving our belongings in. I really liked it because it was so much bigger than the other place and I imagined Luke being there with us too. I sorted out some of our things while I was there.

After we had been in the hospital in Bath for a week or so, we brought Luke home with us for a couple of hours, just to get used to it for him and for us. It was interesting. I felt like I had given birth again and I was taking my newborn baby home – a strange feeling. He was happy and we couldn't wait to show him his toys and just to be a normal family again, spending time at home, not in hospital. After we'd been at home for a short time, Luke's NG tube came out and so we had to go back a bit sooner than intended for a nurse to replace it. But overall we were confident and couldn't wait to have him for longer.

We tried having him at home for a night as well. Luke had an oxygen saturation probe, so just like in hospital we set up the parameters for the loud alarm which would wake us up if there was a problem. We were always awake when he made little sounds like a little baby anyway, and just got used to getting up when he needed us. Finally, after four months in three hospitals, we were able to leave our local hospital as well. We were happy and Luke was happy too.

Luke had a new cot just like in hospital, which made his tracheostomy care much easier as we could set the cot to the right height to be able to reach him. The bed also tilted, allowing him to sleep at an angle rather than on the flat, for his shunt and to reduce the chance of reflux. Our CLIC social worker, whom we'd met in hospital in Bristol, came to visit us at home and talked about the needs in Luke's care, breaks for us like holidays, hospice, grants, funds, petrol money etc. I was grateful to feel we had so much support. Luke was eligible for a disabled person's blue badge which made parking much easier. When we had to go to hospital in Bristol we were able to park in the very limited hospital car parks free of charge.

When my maternity leave came to its end, I gave up my job and became Luke's carer – there was no way I could return to work or take him to the nursery in these circumstances.

Ally and Sarah came to take blood weekly, or more often if needed, and if we had to go to the hospital it wasn't a problem as we lived really close – only ten minutes' walk door to door. We still had to go to hospital frequently for chemotherapy and other appointments.

Luke was becoming more active; he wanted to sit up and eventually, when he was eleven months old, he accomplished it. This was the result of a lot of practice and encouragement through daily physiotherapy sessions back when he was in the hospital in Bristol. He clapped and you could see on his face how proud he was of himself. I cried tears of joy as I did whenever he did something new. We needed to have cushions on the floor all around him as he was a bit wobbly but he enjoyed sitting. He started to wave happily when James went to work or came home. He was so into balls and loved playing with them all the time. He had lots of toys but he wasn't very interested in playing with them; balls took preference. He started to be able to make little sounds when he was excited, like when he saw a balloon or something he liked, which was delightful to hear.

From his time in hospital Luke's musical gift really became apparent. My dad and my brother Matyi both used to play the drums, and Matyi writes music as well. Luke loved musical instruments and when he listened to music he danced and clapped. As you may recall, Luke had always moved a lot when I was pregnant and played the piano. He now quickly got used to playing the piano with his tiny fingers and, as he grew older, would learn to concentrate on the playing. Rather than just hitting the keys or being loud, it was as if he would be improvising. He wouldn't let us play when sitting at the piano with him; he always pushed our hands away. It was quite funny. He moved as he played and also made a sound as though he was singing.

Luke started to communicate more. When something happened, like James dropped something accidentally on the floor, he put his left hand on his head and said, "Uh oh." He also learned how to sign "finished" with his hands. He gradually picked up more and more signing which was impressive and encouraging to see.

At the beginning of March 2014, Luke had his first scheduled MRI scan since the operations. The scan showed no change and they carried on with the chemotherapy cycles. It was a great relief and meant that we could plan a little further.

We were very excited to celebrate Luke's first birthday and wanted to share our happiness with lots of friends and family. His chemotherapy was planned to be on his birthday but our consultant said we could start it on the next day instead. However, we just wanted to carry on as normal; Luke had to be in hospital anyway and as a one-year-old he didn't understand it was his birthday. So I made some invitation cards with him, and James did the shopping for party food and drink.

We wanted to hold Luke's party at the Church Centre but it was booked already so we found somewhere else nearby. Then the day before the event, we received an email quite late in the afternoon to say that something had happened with the room booking and we wouldn't be able to have the party there. So we had to think about other options pretty quickly. James called the Church Centre again and, amazingly, we were able to use the main rooms for Luke's party after all as they had had a cancellation.

I asked Luke's cousin Em to make a birthday cake in the shape of Mr Snail, Luke's favourite toy. Em is very skilled at baking cakes. She happily agreed and I couldn't wait to see the finished product. I sent her a few pictures from different angles to remind her what Mr Snail looked like, and just hoped that it wouldn't be too difficult for her. When she finally showed me the cake I was in tears along with Haze; it was incredible! Lots of people took pictures of the cake and Mr Snail together and you could hardly see any difference between them. When James brought the cake to Luke he wanted to hold it, so I think he loved it. His party was a great success and he received lots of presents from all our friends and family, which he enjoyed opening.

We went to the hospital to have his chemotherapy and his room there was decorated with "Happy Birthday" banners. He received a present from the nurses and from our CLIC nurses. It blessed us to see that they had thought of him.

One day I sat down to think. "My little baby is a year old and time is really flying." I felt so sorry for him that he had had to go through so much and couldn't just live a 'normal' life like other children. But he did the best he could and was happy with everything he achieved, and that kept us going. If I had to cry, I saved it for when I went to bed because he could sense when I was sad and of course I wanted to keep this from him. But I kept praying for his healing and that he would be able to have a long and happy life with us.

The next morning, I was woken by a small noise and discovered that Luke was already sitting up in the cot. I jumped up quickly out of bed and both of us smiled at the same time. "We have to be careful now, mister!" I laughed.

We never became bored as there were many visitors all the time – friends and family, and medical professionals. Mum and I took Luke on lots of walks. And we received deliveries of his special feed and tracheostomy supplies.

Every fourth chemotherapy was in Bristol and Luke needed to stay in for three or four nights for this. Each time we went, the nurses were amazed to see how much he had changed – how he had grown and what he could do. At least the ward was familiar for us – the same ward where Luke had stayed for a couple of months over the previous winter – and we knew all the nurses and doctors.

Because the regional neuro-specialist team had moved from Frenchay Hospital, due to its recent closure, to the Children's Hospital, it was easy for them to come up and see Luke while he was an inpatient. They offered a neuro-rehabilitation which meant two or three weeks of intensive physiotherapy and speech and language therapy on the neuro-rehabilitation ward. This didn't mean we would be stuck in the hospital; if we wanted we could leave the hospital for a night and for the weekend, as long as we were there all day every weekday for the sessions. So they put us on the waiting list but someone came to restart his speech and language therapy while he was staying on the oncology ward. Sometimes Luke wasn't interested but when the therapist showed him her iPad and a pond app with fish he became very excited and couldn't stop tapping on it. She was very impressed with Luke's signing, just as we were.

Luke didn't sleep very well during this particular stay in hospital because of his temperature and he had been sick a lot as well. But something amazing happened on May 4th. It was the middle of the night. I had to change Luke's tracheostomy dressing because he had vomited on it. I called the nurse to help but Luke was very tired and didn't want anyone to touch him. During the dressing change he was sick again and we had to sit him up quickly; then, out of nowhere, he shouted loudly, "ANYA!"

The nurse asked, "What was that and what does it mean?"

I cried as I held him and helped him calm down. It was the most beautiful word that I never thought I would be able to hear from Luke. "Mummy."

The nurse laughed, "Wow, Luke, how could you manage to say this while you're being sick too?"

I explained that it was the first time he'd said anything. Ever since then, he has called me "Anya", which is so special because it's a word in my language, Hungarian.

While we were in the hospital Luke had his tracheostomy review again which involved him going into theatre under a general anaesthetic and the surgeon looking around his airway with a camera. It showed that he couldn't completely close over his airway to swallow, so we didn't push him with purées as we had to be careful where the purée went.

He also had some granulations, growths on the side of his trachea, which needed to be removed during the next review, or before if they started to bleed. They didn't change the tracheostomy size, which we had hoped for in order to wean him off using the tracheostomy, and they said they wouldn't remove the granulations while he was on chemotherapy. Because he was sick so often he needed a safe airway that only the tracheostomy could provide.

Being in hospital for a month this time, we suggested to my mum that she would take this opportunity to go back to Hungary to have a little break. James was at work during the daytime and came to see us in the hospital after work and at weekends. The sad thing was that Luke wasn't allowed to go out of his room as he had to be kept in infectious isolation. We were therefore stuck in the room but at least had some floor time so he wasn't in his cot all the time, and we tried to have lots of fun as always.

Finally, his high temperature was gone, he recovered from the virus, he had a blood transfusion to top up his red blood cells, and we were ready to go home. However, this would only be for one night as he was due to be in hospital in Bath for a few days for chemotherapy starting the next day. I asked our doctor in Bath whether the tumour could return while he was on chemotherapy. She considered it unlikely, but said it would be best not to think of this happening.

CHAPTER EIGHT

An Unwelcome Surprise

BRISTOL CHILDREN'S HOSPITAL

*There are secret things that belong to the Lord our God, but the
revealed things belong to us and our descendants forever, so that
we may obey these words of that law.*

Deuteronomy 29:29

A t the end of June, Luke had his next quarterly MRI scan. It was a long week's wait for us as we didn't hear any news. On July 1st, James came home around lunchtime, which was a big surprise. He asked Mum to look after Luke while he took me into our bedroom to talk with me. In turned out he had received a phone call the previous day and been informed that the doctors had found something and wanted to talk to us about it today. I burst into tears and asked him why he hadn't let me know straightaway. He explained that he knew I wouldn't have been able to sleep at night – and he was right. I told Mum we would all need to go to Bristol; she would be able to look after Luke while we talked with his consultant.

When we arrived, we went into one of the rooms and sat on the bed. One of the CLIC nurses, Ally, was there too and I could see that her face was not the usual happy, smiley one. Our consultant said that Luke had a small tumour growing in the centre of his brain. They were not sure that they could treat it and it was best to stop the chemotherapy as the cancer had broken through it already; clearly, the treatment was ineffective against Luke's aggressive cancer type. Due to the location of the tumour, an operation would be really dangerous for him.

They wanted to make sure that it was a cancerous growth and to see what kind of tumour, so the plan was to come back for a biopsy. For this, they would use the ommaya reservoir that had earlier been inserted into the top of his head, to go down into the middle of his brain. If the biopsy showed it was not actually cancer, then Luke would need to go back on to chemotherapy as quickly as possible. If it was cancer, then there was the option of stereotactic radiotherapy[20] to shrink the tumour down and extend Luke's life.

I could hardly say anything and I couldn't stop crying. We asked how long Luke had to live and of course there was no real answer, just "months". They encouraged us to enjoy every day with him and create lots of happy memories while we could.

We came home with questions, such as what to do next. Luke saw my sadness and stroked my face. I couldn't sleep at all that night. I just cried and was overwhelmed by the fear of death; a sense of emptiness came over me. What was I going to do without him? What had we done to deserve this and where was God in all this?

From this point onwards we started to make plans for every single day – what we wanted to do and where we wanted to go, to try and "do more things". It was hard because we didn't know what Luke wanted to do, as he was only seventeen months old, but we tried our best. It felt strange having another change in routine – no longer visiting the hospital regularly for chemotherapy – but Ally and Sarah kept visiting us weekly to take blood. I cried and asked what

---

[20] targeted radiotherapy, also called radiosurgery

symptoms we should look out for that would indicate the end was approaching, but at the same time I didn't want to talk about it as I made myself so upset. Sarah talked about Charlton Farm Children's Hospice and asked if we would go with her and have a look at it. I thought it would be a terrible place where children go to spend their last days, but I gave it a go. We arranged a short visit for one day the following week, and Sarah came too.

It was in a hidden location in the countryside and I immediately liked it. The staff were amazing; kind and friendly people who looked after you and your child. There was lovely home-cooked food and great facilities. They didn't ask you things if they could see you didn't want to talk, and they understood what you were going through. They could also look after your child if you left for a few days – or you could stay there as well. We decided to come back soon and stay for one night to see how it would go.

Our CLIC social worker came and spoke to us about a number of charities that could arrange a holiday for us; if we wanted to go we just needed to let her know.

We had to go to Bristol several times to meet with various doctors and for Luke to have the lumbar puncture[21] to check if any cancerous cells were flowing in the CSF, and then for the biopsy. We went to the neuro ward in Bristol and spoke with his surgeon, who explained the biopsy procedure in more detail. It didn't take long and Luke was back to his normal self quite quickly, but we had to stay in for a few days so they could keep him under observation. We went home after a few days and nervously waited for the result.

Later that week, on a lovely, bright summer's Friday evening, we went to the park with my brother and watched the hot air balloons rise into the air. Luke really enjoyed that. He wanted to grab hold of them as he thought they were just like his balloons at home.

James received a phone call. It was the hospital and we thought it must be the result of the biopsy so he walked off a little distance to concentrate on the call. It was the neurosurgeon. He apologised that there had been a tremendous error. The tissue removed during the biopsy had been sent to the wrong lab and had had the wrong

---

[21] inserting a needle into the spine to draw some fluid

treatment; essentially, it was by now unusable. Because of this the whole biopsy would need to be done again.

The neurosurgeon was very apologetic, even though it wasn't his fault personally. He was due to go away on holiday the next week so he suggested that the biopsy could be retaken the following morning, Saturday. He asked us to decide and let him know by half past eight that night.

By coincidence, when we got back to the car we bumped into Luke's Bath doctor and told her what had happened. She couldn't believe it either but encouraged us that if he had coped well with it the previous time, he should cope well with doing it again. So we called the surgeon back with our assent.

Early the following morning we returned to the hospital. While Luke was in the recovery room the surgeon came with one of the medical directors of the hospital to apologise for what had happened previously and they told us they would report it as a serious incident and investigate thoroughly.

"This is a joke," I replied, exasperated. "Is it not enough that we are going through this situation with Luke? Taking the biopsy twice is just too much."

This time Luke was rather shaky and got a slight temperature, which is common, so we stayed in for a few days. We had noticed a few weeks earlier that his right eye followed the left eye less than it had before. In addition, he kept pushing his eye with his finger, especially when he was tired, and the doctor said it could be because of the nerves and the tumour there giving him an altered sensation.

We went home and a few days later returned to Bristol for a meeting with our consultant and a radiotherapy consultant. She talked about radiosurgery, the targeted radiation called 'gamma knife'. Because the tumour had been small to start with and had been reduced in size due to the two biopsies being taken, it wouldn't be worth trying to remove surgically. We still hadn't got the biopsy result back but they were ninety percent sure it was a metastasis from the initial tumour. They reminded us it had already been aggressive when they had first diagnosed Luke and this tumour could come back anytime and anywhere in his brain. After the radiotherapy they could discuss further treatment such as a new chemotherapy protocol which could be oral or intravenous, given daily.

"This is all too much!" I exclaimed. If there was no cure and the chemotherapy didn't work, I didn't want to poison my son anymore; I just wanted to be with him as long as I could without any strong medication. I felt so angry that in the long run the medical profession could not do anything for my son; they just kept apologising. I was incredibly upset and disappointed; how on earth, and why, does this nasty disease exist and poor little children have to die without hardly experiencing life?

I kept trying to think of alternatives, and many people got in touch to suggest alternative treatments but I found them pointless. I didn't want to spend thousands of pounds on 'miracle drugs', 'special water', or seeing a healer, when these things didn't have the research to back up their claims. I had to trust in God, that he had a plan, he knew what he was doing and he wanted me to open my eyes. I felt sure he wanted to reveal something to me that I couldn't yet see or understand.

James reduced his hours at work to be with Luke more; he only worked three days a week. He found it very difficult not to be with him as he still continued developing and doing new things, such as starting to crawl and saying more words, albeit it words that only we understood. His speech was not clear but we knew what he was learning and were able to understand him quicker than others. The fact he had started to learn to sign made it much easier for him to communicate with us.

On July 24th, Luke had his radiotherapy. We took him into the room where the procedure would take place and I saw someone preparing the large metal frame – something I don't think I wanted to see. They explained that the frame would be screwed into his head to keep him in exactly the right position and it wouldn't do him any harm. We said our goodbyes to him, kissed his forehead as usual and waited for him on the oncology daybeds ward.

The radiotherapy didn't take a long time and they said it had all gone well. Luke was stable and we were able to go home after a while. He had four little plasters around his head because of the frame. They wanted us to keep the plasters on for a few days, but we noticed there was some fluid leaking out. We called the doctor to discuss it and she said it was normal but that if a lot started to leak then we needed to call her back. Luke was actually fine and fortunately wasn't in any pain that day.

They later told us that Luke was the first child to have this treatment in Bristol and by far the youngest child that any of the team had worked with at other hospitals. One of their main concerns had been how tightly to screw the frame into his skull without fracturing it. Luckily, no damage was caused but the scars from the screws remained visible for months.

It was difficult that we couldn't plan ahead much and didn't know when the worst was coming. I desperately wanted to take Luke to Hungary again but we found out he wasn't able to fly because of his operations. It was really sad that we couldn't go but I reassured my dad that we would sort something out.

James and I had a serious discussion about Luke's future; it was so hard to believe he wouldn't have much of one in this life. I wanted to be sure that God would take care of him and we wanted to dedicate him to God. We didn't want to christen him, mainly because we believe in adult baptism, but also we didn't know who Luke's godparents could be and we didn't want to create pressure for the future. We told Patrick our plan and he was happy to do the dedication for us and, I am sure, for God. We set a date and sent out invitations to friends and family, and we invited my dad and my younger brother Bence to come over from Hungary.

Luke's dedication was very special, although he didn't like it when Patrick put the oil on his forehead – but he did well. He was clapping during the service. Mandy said a lovely prayer for him which touched me so much. Then I had a slight warm, shaky sensation, like a rush of relief. From this point on I knew that Luke was going to be fine.

After the dedication we shared a lovely lunch together with lots of our friends and family, and while my dad and Bence were in England we made sure to spend quality days together, so we kept ourselves busy with a few day trips.

By this time, James had decided he couldn't continue at work any longer so he left. He didn't want to miss out on precious time with Luke; doing three days wasn't working and he needed to be available any time for us to go to hospital and for Luke's appointments. It also meant that we could do more with the time we had because we could go places by car that were unreachable for Luke, Mum and me to get to by foot. It was a difficult decision financially but James said Luke was more important than money and working was not a priority in this situation we were in. We started to do more fun things and continue our 'holiday' life. If Luke wasn't going to have a large quantity of days ahead of him, then we wanted him to have quality days and show him as many things as we were able to. We bought season memberships for Bristol Zoo, Bristol Aquarium, National Trust and Avon Valley Country Park. So then anytime we were in Bristol for an appointment, or just wanted to head out, we could pop in and see the animals.

We knew that Luke loved fish and he made fish noises with his mouth when he saw pictures of fish in books or saw any real ones, such as when we had a trip to the local garden centre just to see fish. So James and I surprised him with two baby goldfish – one was actually gold, the other only half gold in colour. We had never had fish before and had no idea about how to care for them but of course we were happy to do everything for Luke. James took charge of getting everything we needed and cleaning the fish tank. It took ages to decide what to call them, but Luke's cousin Josh had the idea to call them "Fish" and "Chips", which we liked. They were very fitting names!

Luke loved them and each day he said goodnight to them when he went to bed. Mum fed them in the morning and Luke would sign to show that 'Eri Mama' was feeding them, in his funny way.

We were put in touch with a charity that connects families like us with generous hoteliers who have a spare room for a free holiday. They arranged a week in Devon for us in August. This was to be our first time going away since Luke had become ill; the only places we had stayed were the hospital in Bath and the Children's Hospital in Bristol. So we had to pack very carefully and take all of our 'mini hospital' from home, making sure we had sufficient supplies of all Luke's medical and feed things.

We had a lovely week in Devon. When we checked in and went to our room, there was a special welcome pack waiting for us, with free tickets to local attractions, vouchers for free cream teas and meals, and so on. We were treated very well. There was a church group staying in the hotel too, seemingly all above retirement age, and they held services every single morning before breakfast; we joined them on one occasion. We also met a family who had lost their child a few years ago and were also benefiting from the special holiday so they had time together as a family. Every evening there was entertainment provided; and as the lounge was very close to our room we heard most of it whether we attended in person or not. I went to a bingo night one evening while James looked after Luke while he slept, which was fun.

We had an opportunity to meet up with the family of Leah, the girl who had been in the adjacent room to Luke in Bristol Children's Hospital, since she lived in Devon. It was really good to see them and catch up with how they were doing. I loved her mum Jo's positive attitude for her and for her family. That's how I felt too. I became stronger and stronger each day and didn't want to let myself get down for Luke's sake.

We also met up with some of James' friends and went to see Haze and her family. Because they live by the seaside, we had a lovely time at the beach with them and enjoyed some delicious ice cream.

We appreciated almost every minute of our holiday. We took many pictures and even made a holiday memory scrapbook.

Luke's development amazed us all. He started to say, "Ma-mamama," and could soon call both of his grandmas "Mama", which is the Hungarian for 'Grandma'. I had to give up his hand and foot printing as he didn't like paint or anything 'dirty' touching his skin. He wasn't into craft at all, but he was good with books and pointing to animals, building bricks and throwing balls.

In September Luke's next MRI scan was due and we wanted to see whether the radiotherapy had been successful. We didn't want to have to go the following week and sit down to go through the result again, so we asked to get the results by phone, which also meant we could receive them sooner. When we finally received the call there was both good news and bad news. The good news was that the tumour treated with radiotherapy was gone. The bad news was that a new tumour was now growing where the original had been, as if it had come back, on the back of his head.

Following our chats a few months back when they had told us about the previous tumour breaking through the chemotherapy, I had half expected to hear this, so it wasn't entirely shocking. But it was surprising how quickly it had happened. It was really early. He was off the chemotherapy and the only medication he was taking was anti-sickness, but I just kept wondering, how fast can this tumour grow? James and I spent a few days thinking about the treatment options the doctors presented. I didn't want to hear it. I kept saying, "If Luke hasn't got long left, whatever else they do may poison him now and damage him further. Let's just leave him alone to live as happily as he is now."

We had a few days away to stay with Grandad Martin and to go to Uncle Rich's birthday party. Then we went to Cardiff to see Eszter and Balint and to visit everyone at our old church, Mack, where James and I had met each other. They gave us a warm welcome.

We went about life as normally as we could but James kept asking me what we should do now. I desperately prayed and ask God the same question.

Our Bristol oncology consultant phoned to invite us to have a chat with him so we went to Bristol. He presented some options about a chemotherapy drug called etoposide which can be given daily orally or an alternative that could be given intravenously daily in hospital. The two options had different protocols but they were something like twenty-one days on, seven days off.

This chemotherapy wasn't aiming to be curative, but could maybe slow down the cancer cells' growth. I felt very disappointed because the first chemotherapy hadn't worked and to hear that this "might help" wasn't really helpful in making a decision. Also we had a chat with the radiotherapy consultant about having a six-week course of radiotherapy to slow the tumour's growth down. This didn't help me either. I didn't want him to go through more radiotherapy.

They also mentioned a medicine used for epilepsy called Sodium Valproate. Luke didn't suffer from epilepsy but in the US they had some early research showing it may help target the kind of brain tumours Luke had. They said it was a frequently used medicine and it wouldn't do any harm to him; it's not a strong drug. Also, the chemotherapy suggested was quite mild and probably wouldn't cause any side effects like losing his hair, although it might possibly thin out, and it would not make him too nauseous. The difficult balance was to extend his life but also strive for quality of life.

I needed more time to think about the options and we had more trips and meet-ups with people.

Then I heard a voice say, "Everything will be fine." It was the voice that I hadn't heard for ages, and the voice that I really wanted to hear. I knew that God was looking after Luke and still working on me.

I told James I agreed with starting the Sodium Valproate, so we did. Then he asked me, "What about the radiotherapy?"

"No way!" I replied.

After hearing such side effects as memory loss, difficulties with maths and counting, I didn't want to damage Luke's brain. He was so normal and clever and I was worried he would lose his skills. But then a few days later I finally agreed, "Let's do it." I hadn't really changed my opinion but felt under pressure from James – he truly believed it was the best thing for our son.

We had to go for an appointment in radiotherapy, where they made Luke's mask while he was under a general anaesthetic, and this would be used each day to ensure he was lying in the right position. They explained that it was a six-week course, early every morning from Monday to Friday; we had to be there at 8am. However, we wanted to avoid travelling so much, particularly with the morning traffic, so we arranged to stay in CLIC House[22] near the hospital and to go home for the weekends.

The radiotherapy started on October 16th, and every day Luke had to go under general anaesthetic as it was impossible for him to lie perfectly still for fifteen minutes – and of course he would have cried a lot and needed suctioning. James and I waited by the recovery room until we were able to go and see him. Each day of the week he had a different anaesthetist, and most days we could go into the recovery room before he woke up, but hard as it was, we had to respect the rules and the anaesthetist's decision if they didn't want us in the room until he woke up. We were desperate to be there and for him to see us when he opened his eyes, and also we didn't trust anyone to take care of his tracheostomy well enough.

Luke coped really well during these weeks except that his poor ears got very burnt from the radiation; we amply applied aqueous cream every day as soon as we noticed. Unfortunately, they hadn't warned us about this before he started the radiotherapy, otherwise we

---

[22] a property for families of children receiving oncology treatment

could have begun using the cream earlier. It seems from our conversations with other parents of children who've had this treatment that they were not told either – surprising as it is something so basic. Generally, we had to rely on ourselves to work out what was needed as we went along.

Each day after the radiotherapy treatment, Luke had to go up to the oncology day beds ward for an hour to make sure he was OK following the general anaesthetic and sometimes he had blood taken to check his levels. When we were finished in hospital, by ten o'clock, we usually had time to go out for a quick activity before returning to CLIC House for his midday sleep. We also went out most afternoons to places like the zoo, aquarium or the city farm to see the "guys" (that's what we called the animals; I think it came from Justin on Something Special first). We made sure Luke was coping well and at the same time had fun with him.

Once when we went to see Luke in the recovery room, I took him from the arms of the nurse who had been holding him, and his tracheostomy sound was a bit strange. We thought it was just because of the general anaesthetic as often it was a little blocked or dry, so we said we would sort it out when we got up to the ward. I carried him as usual to Day Beds in my arms and then took a look to find out what was wrong. It turned out that the tube was out of his tracheostomy for the first time ever. We had to grab our emergency tracheostomy kit, which we carried with Luke at all times, to put it back in. The nurse said she would need to report this and of course we agreed as we didn't want it to happen again. From this point on, the first thing we did each day when we got to Luke in the recovery room was to check his tracheostomy. The staff apologised but it wasn't really enough.

On the last Friday of radiotherapy (the final treatment was the following Wednesday because we had started on a Thursday), just as we were looking forward to going home from Bristol for the weekend, Luke's temperature rose. As per the protocol, he needed to start intravenous antibiotics so we ended up on the oncology ward for the weekend. As usual, the nurses took swabs from his nose, tracheostomy and groin, and the tests showed he had a viral infection at the tracheostomy; but he felt fine and his temperature quickly returned to normal.

It was during this weekend that Luke started to 'send kisses'. It was delightful to see how he was developing emotionally; he learned new skills so quickly. Also during this stay we met the Hungarian doctor Daniel again, and it was good to catch up.

We were discharged on the Sunday afternoon, so were able to return home for the rest of the day but had to go back to Bristol the next day for radiotherapy. Then a few days later it was all finished. However, we would have to wait until January for the next MRI scan to see what difference the radiotherapy had made, since the radiation continues to work for several weeks after the treatment has been given.

I couldn't believe it had finally finished and we could go back to normal again. The past few weeks had been very difficult for us and had put pressure on our marriage too. We had spent too long being together but without concentrating on one another. Luke was the priority and I felt we were in a race or a competition with respect to his care. James always took over and I felt under pressure that I was not doing everything well enough for Luke. I didn't feel like I was able to mother him because James wanted to do everything for him as quickly as he could. But whenever Luke cried, James passed him over to me because he couldn't calm him down. James takes care of the practical side well but I understand Luke better. Sometimes he didn't want to play – he just wanted to lie on me – but then James would ask why we weren't playing, saying Luke was bored. He always wanted to keep him busy but I didn't believe that was the right approach. James is quite an active person and gets into action fast, whilst I am calm and think matters through before I start anything.

So we began to argue a lot and I didn't know what was needed for our marriage to survive – or whether it could survive at all. Sometimes I didn't speak to him at all, and I felt fine about that because if we started to talk it would just turn into an argument. We only discussed basic matters about Luke. We didn't do much together as a couple; the two of us were almost never able to go out. There were two occasions when we had dinner out, when James' mum came to visit and we left Luke with her and my mum. But all we could talk about all the time was Luke. We rushed through our meals and went home quickly to check that everything was OK.

All this was compounded by the fact that James wasn't working. We were together 24/7 which made it even more difficult. So I had other matters to pray about besides Luke's wellbeing.

By now it was the end of November. We hadn't wanted to focus on Christmas plans – everyone kept asking us what we were doing and where we would be – because we didn't know if Luke would be with us.

We enjoyed making a few long journeys, to meet Auntie Haze and the children and another time to see Uncle Rich and his family, where we would meet halfway. We always had lovely days out.

Luke was crawling a lot and he also enjoyed walking with support under his armpits. He started to call for me – "Anya!" – more clearly when he really wanted me. It was amazing to hear this each day. As he crawled to my mum's room he called out for her too: "Mama!"

Luke had a tracheostomy review with the ENT surgeon under general anaesthetic, where they looked around his airway with a camera. After a while, one of the nurses came to let us know that he was in the recovery room. James and I set off but the nurse insisted on only one parent being allowed in, even though James explained that normally we both went in so we were able to care for his tracheostomy.

So I entered the recovery room and saw Luke lying on his side in the bed, and I immediately noticed that he had a new tracheostomy tube in. The staff said they had changed the tube for a smaller one, a size down – he'd had size four before – but this tube was a completely different type from what he'd had up until now. I wanted to straighten him out in the middle of the bed to open his airway for him as the tube was being blocked by his chin and I could hardly see the hole.

As soon as I moved Luke to the middle of the bed I noticed the tube was out of the stoma. I can't explain how angry I was, and I started to shout that the tube was out and I needed help. It was a tiny one and the fabric tapes were hardly holding it. So I cut the tapes, which enabled me to put it back. By this time Luke had started to wake up and I needed to suction him as the tube was filling with secretions.

I asked a nurse to help while I was holding the tube, trying to calm Luke down. She passed me the catheter, saying I could do it better than her, but I shouted back something like, "How on earth can I suction him while I am holding the tube?" – I needed someone else to hold it for me while I suctioned. I felt straightaway that the vacuum setting was wrong so I instructed her twice to reduce the pressure, with her asking, "Is that better?" To make matters worse, it was a different size of catheter as well. Then I needed new tapes to hold the tracheostomy tube and I said, "Ours are in the emergency bag over there," and someone passed them to me. Those few minutes were a nightmare.

When we came out James saw the anger on my face and asked what had happened. I told him that the tracheostomy tube had come out again and how the nurses had been helpless. We knew that this new type of tube wouldn't be safe for Luke because his chin kept pushing off the Swedish nose and blocking the tube, and also we didn't have any smaller suction catheters that were needed to fit the size three tube.[23]

The nurses told us not to worry and that our community nurses would provide us with the supplies we needed. But we told them this is not how it works; due to the fact they only place orders and receive deliveries once a week, it would take ten days to get us the catheters, and we clearly couldn't go home without any, when Luke was using fifty per day on average.

We asked for an extended tube in this new size but they said they didn't have any of the type we were used to. So we had no choice but to change the tube for a 3.5 one from Luke's emergency bag, smaller than his previous tube but larger than the one they had just put in.

When we had calmed down, James asked to speak to the ward sister. He said he was going to make a formal complaint about this incident and to make sure staff in the recovery room were trained with tracheostomy care. We also wanted it put in writing that both of us were to be with Luke in the recovery room whenever he woke up from a general anaesthetic, firstly in case of any problems such as those we'd experienced twice (as it needs two people to put the tracheostomy tube in and secure it), and secondly because Luke's

---

[23] The size number is the internal diameter in millimetres so size three is much smaller than size four

general tracheostomy care such as suctioning meant it is necessary to have both of us there – one to comfort him and one to suction.[24]

Shortly after, Christmastime came and, as usual, Eszter and Balint visited us on December 23rd. We spent the next few days with my brother, James' mum and of course my mum, who was still living with us. Luke helped me to decorate the Christmas tree. He didn't know what was going on or what all the wrapping paper was about. We wanted to make this Christmas extra special as we realised it could be his last.

One of my friends from church whom I had got to know at the baby group had a lovely little daughter a little older than Luke called Evelyn, and around this time she become seriously ill. She had to go to Bristol Children's Hospital and was on ventilation. I kept in touch with her mum, Sarah, and told her we were praying for her and would see her when we were next at hospital. It was hard, and very strange, to be in the paediatric Intensive Care Unit again and see her on the machine. I recognised one of the nurses and smiled; I felt Evelyn was in good hands. She was suffering from a very rare illness called HDH. They treated her with chemotherapy. I had never heard of chemotherapy being used as a treatment for anything other than cancer or leukaemia before. It was a good feeling that this time I could care for someone else, rather than people caring for us. So we packed some food and drink up and took it in when we saw them.

We were getting close to the next scan in January 2015. On the day of the scan, we waited for a very long time but eventually they told us the MRI scanner had broken and so we'd have to go back the following week for the appointment. Luke coped well with the general anaesthetic and I went up to visit Evelyn on the ward again when he had finished. The nurses recognised me straightaway and were excited to hear any news about Luke. Evelyn looked much better, although weak, but the steroids she was having were making her hungry all the time. Sarah was expecting her second baby

---

[24] The result of this complaint was an action plan and letter of apology to a certain extent. One of the things proposed was that we would complete the Hospital Passport which would detail all of Luke's diagnoses, cares, supplies, likes and dislikes to ensure better treatment in hospital in the future. We did this, but it didn't appear to be used by staff as they didn't seem to know some of the key information we provided in the Passport.

daughter so I congratulated her; her mum came to stay with them so she could take little breaks.

A week later we had a phone call about Luke's scan result. The six-week radiotherapy hadn't been successful and the tumour had kept growing. We had to have a serious conversation with the consultant again about the options at this stage, and how to control the growth. They wanted Luke to have a lumbar puncture. This involved another general anaesthetic but of course he was used to it by now. Afterwards the doctor came to explain that the procedure hadn't been successful, so we had to come back again the following week. This time it went well and the result was that there weren't any cancer cells in the sample taken.

A few days later we travelled up to the Midlands for Luke's cousin George's birthday party, and we stayed at Grandad's (James' dad's home). Luke didn't enjoy the party at all; he really didn't like the noise of so many people and after a while when we realised he wasn't actually going to stop being frightened and crying, we had to go into a quiet side room for the remaining hours of the party. But overall we enjoyed our time there.

We decided to start the oral chemotherapy[25] which we hoped would control the growth. It would be twenty-one consecutive days 'on' and seven days 'off' to allow his body to recover, before starting another cycle again.

We had a meeting with the neurosurgeon who'd carried out most of the previous operations. He thought he could remove the tumour without causing too much damage. We had never expected major brain surgery to be something Luke would have to face again so we had to think about it, but we didn't have long to reach a decision as he wanted to perform the operation soon.

The next week, Mum went back to Hungary for a visit and I really wanted Dad to come back with her when she returned, even just for a few days before the operation, which we had by now consented to. They arrived on Tuesday, two days before the operation was scheduled, and we collected them from the airport between various hospital appointments – three in total that day.

---

[25] etoposide

Haze wanted to see Luke before the operation and she drove all the way to Bristol Airport to see us while we waited for my parents to arrive off the plane. She brought two lovely animal books and Luke enjoyed reading them with her and pointing.

Luke enjoyed a couple of special days with my dad, and they had a few nice music sessions together. Luke is so into music; he loves all types of musical instruments.

CHAPTER NINE

Miracles Do Happen

How beautiful are the feet of messengers who bring good news!
Romans 10:15

Faith comes from hearing, that is, hearing the Good News about Christ.

Roman 10:17

God saved you by his grace when you believed. And you can't take credit for this; it is a gift from God.

Ephesians 2:8

Each evening when I put Luke to sleep, I prayed with him for other children we met in the hospital, for ill children in the world, for family and friends, and for Luke himself. Before this operation, I prayed and then said to Luke, "God loves you so much; he is looking after you and he made you strong." Luke hadn't seen the sign for 'strong' before and probably hadn't heard the word all that much. But when I said, "God made you strong," he clenched his fists, lifted them up and made the noise of trying to speak the word. He also repeated the word 'amen' after me. I had a warm, shaky feeling and knew it was the Holy Spirit. I was calmer than usual and the fear of death had been taken away from me. I knew that if anything happened to Luke, he would be fine with God. I wasn't afraid of the coming operation; I gave all my worries to God and I knew Luke would be fine in his hands.

On Thursday, we set off very early with the car full of bags and boxes – even though we were going to a hospital, we had to take many medical supplies with us because they didn't have the right ones, or enough of them – to take Luke for his operation. Luke had a little cuddle time with 'Ocsi Papa' (my dad) and we said goodbye as he was going back to Hungary two days later and we didn't know if we would see him. We went through the usual procedures – settling in, paperwork, a visit from the anaesthetist – and we then set about waiting for them to call us down to theatre. Poor Luke had to be starved for the anaesthetic and he seemed hungry as we spent hours waiting, trying to keep him entertained.

Eventually at around midday, the neurosurgeon came and told us he had to reschedule the operation because the intraoperative MRI scanner had broken. This scanner was very important as it would allow them to see during the operation if any tumour was remaining or if there was more to be removed. In Britain there are only two of these scanners and fortunately this new one was in Bristol. They told us they had ordered the required part from Germany which would be flown over to arrive the next day. However, as the MRI scanner would only be needed in the later stages of the operation, they planned to begin operating earlier that day, if we were happy to go ahead. The part would arrive and be fitted by an engineer while the operation was taking place. We agreed to this.

So we unexpectedly got to go home and spend a bit more time with Ocsi Papa. It was also my brother Matyi's birthday, so at least he didn't need to worry about Luke the whole day. That was just another sign from God; to have some family time together without worrying was really good.

The next day we went back to the hospital. Fortunately, we had been able to keep most of Luke's bags and boxes in the room, but even so we still had plenty of things to take in with us when we arrived at seven the next morning. Luke went to theatre at about nine in the morning and we said our goodbyes and kissed his forehead as always. I knew that God would be with him; there was no doubt in my mind at all. It was good to see the team we had met almost a year-and-a-half previously when Luke had had his initial operations, and everyone remembered him. Moreover, there was a Hungarian neurosurgeon.

We had a long, long day. We waited almost all of the time in Luke's windowless room, hoping for updates, but we did pop out quickly to the hospital shop and coffee shop. One of the anaesthetists came and said Luke was doing well so far and reminded us that his face would be a bit chubby and swollen as he had been lying upside down for the operation. They had also had to change his tracheostomy tube to a plastic one without metal; there was some uncertainty about this prior to the operation, so we wanted to make sure everything was fine, which it was. We thanked the anaesthetist for looking after Luke as he went home and someone else took over from him.

Another surgeon who had been in theatre came and updated us and said that they were finishing up with the operation; they just needed to sew the wound up now. After nine or ten in the evening the surgeon finally came to say that all had gone well and he had been able to remove the whole tumour. He informed us that Luke would need lots of pain relief and that his right side might also be a bit weaker again.

We couldn't wait to see him. However, we had to wait another eternity – three hours passed and we began to worry why it was taking so long. Eventually, at half past one in the morning, we were called to go down to recovery. I can't describe how sad I felt when I saw Luke there. His tongue was an enormous bright red lump, so big that it protruded out of his mouth which he couldn't close because of it. I asked what had happened to him. He was crying but he could hardly make a sound because of his swollen tongue. The medical staff explained that he had been sick in the recovery room, and I wondered whether he might have bitten his tongue when he vomited. The recovery nurses weren't really sure. I felt so sorry for him, whilst simultaneously very upset about what had happened.

Luke wasn't at all comfortable and I couldn't wait to lie down next to him to calm him down. We had taken one of his dummies down to the recovery room for him, as we always did, but there was no way he could use it because of his poor tongue. He had lots of cannulas in him and we didn't know why they hadn't just used his Hickman line which was so easy to use to give medicines or take blood. When we asked, they told us they would use it if they needed to, but they like to have additional 'access'. As well as this he had an arterial line which is used for taking oxygenated blood, rather than blood from veins, and for monitoring blood pressure.

We hardly slept that night. Luke was in so much pain that he wasn't sleeping properly, added to the fact he'd been under anaesthetic sleep all day, and he was given morphine every twenty minutes via the PCA[26]. On the positive side, he was well enough to be in his room in the High Dependency Unit and not be in intensive care and on ventilation, as we had been warned might happen. He coped very well and I was amazed to see what a strong boy I had. He wanted me all the time, which is normal, and he was very sensitive whenever I moved away from him. Almost the only time I could pop out of the room to go to the toilet was when he slept.

The next day I bumped into the anaesthetist and told him about Luke's tongue, which he didn't know about. He couldn't understand what had happened as Luke had been fine when he left him. He promised to come and see him, which he did. In fact, many doctors and nurses came to look at his tongue because they'd heard it was so swollen.

The doctors also arranged for a specialised maxillofacial doctor to check the tongue. He was concerned that when Luke became upset he might bite it again, as it was so large, so he advised us to wedge some sterile gauze into his mouth. It was hard to keep in but we did our best and tried to make sure it stayed clean and healthy. Unfortunately, a few days later Luke's tongue became infected, but at least the swelling had reduced. The right side of his face was a bit weaker again.

The day after the operation, Dad came to say goodbye to us as it was time for him to fly back to Hungary. He hadn't seen Luke after

---

[26] patient controlled analgesia

the initial operations so it was the first time he saw him looking as he did with tubes and cables all over his little body. Dad said it was amazing to observe how strong I was, coping with everything and caring for my son. Luke was sleepy but he could just about manage to wave to Ocsi Papa, which was great to see.

The days ahead were very challenging for us, in fact some of the most difficult of the past few years. Luke's head was swollen for many days. The surgeon said it was normal and that he had expected it to happen, but I didn't remember Luke being so swollen after the first set of operations back in autumn 2013. We were concerned so they arranged a CT scan to check there was no build-up of CSF, and that the shunt which takes excess fluid away from the brain was working properly. It turned out that everything was fine with the shunt and pressure in his brain. But in the night a problem arose. It was three in the morning and one of Luke's cannulas stopped working so they started to use the Hickman line to administer the medicine. Straightaway James noticed that it started to leak the medicine over Luke's chest – it was broken. This meant not only that they didn't have access, but there was also a high risk of infection. Although there had never been any problems with Luke's Hickman line before, James knew exactly what to do. He told the nurse it needed to be clamped immediately, but she wanted to phone the oncology ward to check. James was exhausted – we both were – and perhaps for this reason he didn't feel confident enough to clamp it himself. The nurse returned after a short while and did it.

As the line had been left open and was now only clamped, it wasn't safe for Luke to keep it in. The on-call surgeon came with a Hickman line repair kit – we didn't know they could be repaired! The surgeon and nurse got everything ready and prepared to fix it where we were. However, he had never done this procedure so he actually read the instructions that came with the repair kit right in front of us – very reassuring! When the new end had been carefully slotted into the existing catheter that ran into Luke's chest, he used the special glue to seal the join. The next instruction was that the line shouldn't be used for twenty-four hours. So when they proceeded to test the line by flushing it with saline, it is perhaps unsurprising that the repair job failed. A specialist nurse came the next afternoon to attempt another repair. She said, "If this also fails, the line will have to be removed," and indeed this repair also turned out to be unsuccessful.

Luke started to get temperatures, a symptom of having an infection, and so he needed to have the remaining section of the line removed immediately as it was likely there was a serious bacterial infection on the line itself. The operation to remove it was remarkably short, certainly the fastest operation in his life; it only took half an hour before we were called down to recovery to get him. It felt good to see his naked chest without the line that he'd had in for over a year.

Surprisingly, Luke recovered quite quickly from the main operation and soon we got a bed on the neuro ward. He wanted to sit up all the time so we were able to have some floor time, and he managed a little bit of crawling. He amazed the doctors with his progress and we had regular visits from the oncology doctors too. Luke changed emotionally a lot. He became very sensitive when I left the room, crying a great deal, or even if I shifted my position when lying in bed with him. He wanted me so much to be nearby. I said to James, "I'll just stay with Luke and cuddle him as much as he wants, and you can enjoy being the nurse around us." But when Mum came to visit us I could escape to the toilet quickly as he was fine with her.

I was really happy that we were both allowed to stay in hospital with Luke; usually only one parent is permitted. One night on the neuro ward, I woke up and noticed that he had pulled his tracheostomy tube in the middle of his sleep. I called across to James to wake him up so that he could help me with it. This was the first time Luke had ever pulled out the tube. We had no idea how long it had been out, as his oxygen saturations were fine. The only reason I noticed was that I saw he had pulled his Swedish nose off, so I just thought to check his tube in case it was out, which it was. Such maternal intuition!

Luke was rapidly getting better and better and we wanted to go home again. He had had different medicines prescribed by different doctors and although primarily under the care of the neurologists, the oncology doctors also made their own decisions about his treatment. Unfortunately, a breakdown in communication elongated our stay for a few days but eventually they decided Luke could finish his antibiotic course orally at home instead of needing to stay in to have it intravenously. One of the specialist nurses suddenly came to us at 8pm one evening and said we could go home; we just needed the TTAs[27] which they wouldn't be able to get until the next day. She said we could either go home immediately and come back the next day to get the medicines, or wait until we got them before leaving. It was all very sudden and past Luke's bedtime, and as we weren't packed we decided to stay. We ended up regretting it – we had to wait until 3pm the next day to get the medicines. We learned from this always to leave as soon as possible, and successfully applied this wisdom on future occasions – such as when Luke needed a blood transfusion at our local hospital and they asked us to wait for half an hour. Now we prefer to go home and wait for the medical staff to phone us when the results are ready, because we know that "half an hour" is more likely to be an hour and a half of waiting or even more. When that's added to the three hours that the blood takes to transfuse, it's quite a long time for Luke to be in hospital.

So finally we were able to pack up and go home. We even had just about enough space in the car for Luke's huge fish balloon that James had bought from the aquarium.

For a few weeks and months, he didn't let me go anywhere without him. He cried if he couldn't be on my lap or I went to do something in the kitchen and all the time just called for me – "Anya!" Even when we went out for a walk and James or Mum were pushing instead of me, he became upset because he wanted *me* to push.

He was so sensitive around everyone; he really hated any sudden loud noises like laughing, and he was frightened when people came to visit us at home, especially when he could detect they were medical personnel instead of friends.

It was a tremendously hard time for me because being with James everyday was getting worse and worse. We would argue every single day. I thought it would never end.

A week or so later we went back to Bristol Children's Hospital for Luke to have another operation, this time to replace his Hickman line. We thought he was going to have the same again but at the last minute they offered us the choice between a Hickman line and a Port; we chose the latter, a decision we would later regret.

---

[27] medicines prescribed to take away

The Port is a gel implant that's surgically inserted under the skin and is connected to a major vein running into the heart in the same way as the Hickman line. The main difference is that the Port uses a removable needle so there's only something hanging out of the chest when blood needs to be taken or when intravenous medicines or blood products need to be given. We were supplied with some anaesthetic cream that we needed to apply before using the needle so he wouldn't feel it too much.

We were happy with the Port at first as there wasn't a dressing that needed changing weekly as there had been with the Hickman line, and Luke didn't like that aspect. But at that time we didn't realise he would have finger prick blood samples taken, which we found difficult, as did Luke of course. Although it's only a little pain, he didn't like the squeezing, and the blood came out of his thumbs so slowly that there often wasn't enough to send to the lab anyway. He cried every time one of the CLIC nurses came to take blood, as he knew what was going to happen.

We could leave the Port accessed for a week – which meant there was a needle inserted in the gel, and blood could be taken very easily – and he didn't feel anything. Then afterwards we could de-access the port – removing the needle and line – and you wouldn't have known there was anything there just by looking at his chest.

After having his thumb pricked, when Mum came home from work, Luke always felt sorry for himself and showed his thumb to her and wanted her to kiss it better, even if this was several hours later. This was very amusing.

One day I was cleaning away my books from my bedside table and Luke wanted to grab my bible. He didn't know what the book was and I don't think he had seen me reading it, but he put his hands together and said, "Amen!"

"Unbelievable!" I exclaimed.

Luke just wanted to show me more evidence of God. From then on, whenever we ate he wanted us to say grace; just before we started our food he would put his hands together. Sometimes he was a little distressed but then we would say a quick amen and he would smile. When we prayed before sleep, it was so calm and he loved listening to my prayers. At first he still had a dummy, but then he used to take it out for that minute so that he could concentrate and not be disturbed with the sucking noise. How clever!

Our friends Mandy and Paul gave Luke a lovely book of children's prayers for his dedication and he knew what it was. He said and signed "thank you" whenever he looked at the prayers and pictures on each page.

I was now approaching my thirtieth birthday. Up to this point I hadn't dared to imagine I would be able to celebrate it with my son. Things weren't going well with James but I felt closer and closer to God. I just wanted to be happy on that special day, and in the end I was. In the morning Mandy and I went for a lovely coffee at Bath Priory (a very fine hotel) and had a really good chat. Our church was having a 'prayer week' about the possible development of the church buildings. This meant it was open all day for the week – usually it's not – and it was Mandy's turn to be there for an hour or so. I asked her if I could come along, and we walked around and read the project boards which showed what the church had been like in the past and what might happen in the future. I sat down and started to pray on my own.

"Dear God, thank you that I'm in such a great community, with all the people who are praying for us and for Luke. Thank you for their support, and for all your love and everything you show me about yourself. God, I pray that this church atmosphere will always be the same. Help people to decide what is best for the church and what can be changed in positive ways. I pray that I can be more involved with the church life and could help the community. Please forgive me on my odd days and help me to remain on your path. Lord, I pray for James and for our relationship, that we will see the light in it. I know we are both completely focussed on Luke at the moment but help us to communicate better together and to listen to each other. Please hold Luke in your healing hands and let him be with us. In Jesus' name. Amen."

I felt so well after my prayer. Then I said goodbye to Mandy and thanked her for my coffee and our time together. Eszter and Balint from Cardiff came to see us and we enjoyed a pleasant birthday lunch together at home. It was nice to see them as these days we don't get to meet up with each other very often. My brother came round after he finished work and Mum was there too, so it was very special.

The next day I received an email from Mandy asking if anyone could volunteer on Saturday to help making posies for Mothering Sunday, the following day. "Wow, God," I thought, "that was a quick answer!" So I called the number on the email and said that Mum and I would be happy to help. We had a great time and I enjoyed chatting with the other ladies as we arranged the flowers. I also agreed to organise the Mothering Sunday posies from the following year onwards.

Those months were greatly blessed.

Luke started 'Sing and Sign' classes on Tuesday mornings. He really enjoyed these and his signing improved on almost a daily basis. On the Thursdays we went to Oasis, a baby/toddler and mum Bible study group. I enjoyed it very much. It was good to get to know everyone individually, to pray for others and to be prayed for. On the same day in the evening I started to go to a home group, a Bible study held at someone's home. The people who attended were mainly from the Sunday evening service. I really appreciated this group and liked it when we discussed our thoughts about a story or passage from the Bible and prayed for one other. It felt wonderful that we were all committed to supporting each other.

I found three special Hungarian Christian friends on Facebook – Hajni, Merci and Margit – all of whom live in the UK. We often chatted about God and our lives. In my experience, not many Hungarians reveal their faith; most prefer to hide it. But these three were very special, and it was a blessing to be able to pray for one another. I often asked rhetorically, "Where were you before? Why didn't we find each other earlier?" But God's plan is perfect and he wanted them in my life at this point in time.

Hajni lived in Manchester with her husband Lajos and their young son Bence. Shortly after we met online, she had a second son, Máté, and experienced both his birth and his passing away. Hajni has a deep Christian faith and I was amazed how strong she was when she lost her little boy with a rare genetic condition. It all started when they went to Slovakia to visit her family and for Máté's christening. Hajni went to the family doctor for advice about his lack of movement and unusual breathing. The doctor gave him cough medicine as she noticed he had a cold, and then asked Hajni to come back on the following Monday for a check-up.

That weekend Máté had a high temperature and he was crying a lot and wouldn't settle. The next day the doctor noticed something wasn't right about him and rushed them to hospital. As they arrived and were taking Máté out from the car they noticed mucus coming out from his mouth and nose. They hurried in and the nurse asked them to put him on the couch so that the doctor could examine him. At that exact moment Máté turned grey-purple and stopped breathing. Everybody started rushing around them and Máté was taken away. He was intubated and had a lot of secretions suctioned from his chest. The doctor said although they had successfully stabilised him, he was in a really critical condition and would have to be transferred by ambulance to intensive care in a bigger hospital.

Máté had double pneumonia and one lung wasn't working while the other one was full of secretions. He had to remain on ventilation and his muscles were weak. The family arranged the christening to take place in the hospital.

A medical aeroplane brought Hajni and Máté back to the UK. When they arrived at Royal Manchester Children's Hospital, Máté underwent lots of tests, including genetic analysis of his blood. Then they received the terrible news that he wouldn't be able to make it for much longer. He would live a very short life and had only weeks. He was diagnosed with SMA[28].

Everything happened so fast. I prayed for them earnestly and asked that God would give Hajni strength to cope with everything. Hajni kept the Facebook group of Hungarian friends updated every day about Máté's condition. At one stage it seemed as if he would need a tracheostomy, and I tried to support her by talking about what it was. In the end he didn't have one.

The weekend before he passed away I had a dream in which a little boy – he was actually Prince George – went to heaven with two angels. I clearly saw a light and heard calm voices of angels singing with it. They said that they were going to take him on Tuesday at one in the afternoon.

I told Hajni and the group about my dream. Margit said it didn't mean that Máté was going to die because it was Prince George in the dream, not Máté. I wondered if maybe Prince George was symbolic

---

[28] spinal muscular atrophy type 1

of all children. Margit was really upset about the whole situation and couldn't face what was happening to her friend's son. I was a bit more prepared because of what we had faced with Luke.

It was an extremely difficult time for their family. One week they were celebrating their older child Bence's third birthday and the following week on Tuesday afternoon, with his parents by his bedside, Máté left this world to be in a new, happy and painless eternal life with God.

I am really grateful that I know Hajni and we are able to help each other in different ways. She has a strong faith and I am sure with time God will help her to lessen this big pain.

Relationships are not easy. I know this first-hand; my marriage was close to being finished. James and I had had a bad time. Luke's illness meant so much stress in our everyday life, and it was difficult to separate this from our feelings for each other. Several people generously offered to babysit for Luke so we could go out, but we could not take them up on their kind offers as they wouldn't be able to look after him. On the two or three occasions James and I went out together, leaving Luke in the care of both of our mums, we still didn't leave him for a long time as we worried about what might be happening. Instead, over the months and years we had our breaks separately, doing our own thing. So much of our time was spent with Luke, but we knew we needed to be there for each other as well.

One Sunday morning, the church was very full and there was a busy service with two christenings. Luke was very sensitive to sudden, loud noises and although he usually didn't mind the sounds at church, on this particular day we could tell he didn't feel like being there. James decided to take him home and I would stay at the service; I knew it was Luke's sleep time so he would be fine without me.

For some reason I didn't feel like staying at church either and I left a few minutes after them and turned the other direction, walking up the hill behind the building. As I did so, I began to pray. I told God I couldn't remain in this relationship any more in which I didn't feel like a wife. James and I argued all the time. He just took everything over from me and always wanted to sort things out on his own; he didn't let me be a part of it.

I wanted to be on my own, but as I walked along the path there were lots of people walking their dogs. I cried and asked God, "Why can't I be alone for a little bit? What do you want me to do?"

I looked down from the hill and from far away I spotted James and Luke heading across the sports field to the playground. I couldn't believe I could spot them from so far away. I experienced a warm feeling again and God showed me exactly what I should do. I needed to go back to my family and not let myself get down. James and I needed to try to sort out our feelings and frustrations, and to pray for a better marriage. It's not right to walk out from marriage when things get tough. God doesn't want this to happen. Instead, we can ask him to change us first, and pray for our 'other half' each day. We can do it with his help. To be honest, I hadn't prayed much for us; I was concentrating on Luke all the time. I had let my marriage down.

Before we knew it, it was Luke's second birthday! Luke had a fantastic spotty-themed birthday party at the Church Centre again, in which all the guests had to wear something spotty. It was based on Mr Tumble who likes spotty things, but we broadened it so not everyone would come dressed as Mr Tumble! Luke, however, wore his Mr Tumble spotty clothes and our niece Em made an amazing Mr Tumble birthday cake. We had a bouncy castle as well as some indoor games and I think everyone enjoyed the afternoon. My dad and younger brother Bence flew over to stay with us for a few days.

In the following month, May, we had Luke's next quarterly MRI scan, which showed everything was stable, no changes, and so we were really happy. A stable result always meant we could plan a bit more or do something special. This time we looked forward to going on our church weekend away to Lee Abbey in North Devon. This time we took Mum with us. We wanted her to feel God's Holy Spirit and to show her how special the place was, and she really did. The community members who staff the place are from different countries and we met a few Hungarians as well, which was nice.

When Mum and James took Luke for a walk I had a quiet time to think and pray. I was sitting on the bench there and it was warm, sunny weather. I could see the sea from where I was sitting and there were sheep in the surrounding fields. As I looked at the sky, one of the few clouds formed the image of an angel. I took a picture immediately with my phone.

All weekend I was thinking about my life, the future, and the whole situation with Luke – and then I heard God's whisper. He simply said, "Write it down." So at that time I decided to write this book and record everything about my faith.

My faith was stronger than it had ever been and I felt so excited to start writing. I had a good working pattern; when Luke began his two-hour daily nap, I switched everything off around me and just typed, and I also found time whenever James took Luke out for a few hours.

We had a lovely summer despite the weather and did a lot of activities, including going to South Devon and staying at Mama Pam's and seeing friends while we were down there. We also went to visit our special friend from the hospital, Leah, who wasn't far away. It was good to see how she was getting on.

Then we had a very busy two weeks with my niece who was staying with my brother. Because my brother had to work, we looked after her during the daytime. In fact, we were so busy looking after her all day that it was as if we suddenly had two children. Ninni (Annabella) was a year older than Luke and very active – so different to him with his ever calm nature. Luke loved Ninni being around and they enjoyed playing together. We went out every day to different playgrounds, to see animals at our city farm, and even spent a day at Avon Valley Country Park where there are lots of animals to see and things to play with. While James was walking around with Luke, I had Ninni with me. Ninni went to the petting area and wanted to touch the snake; she is fearless and loves looking at all the animals. She sat down with the other children and took her turn stroking the massive creature, and I was amazed! When she had finished she didn't want to leave the petting barn; she just wanted to touch it again.

A few days later, when Sarah came to take blood from Luke, Ninni started confidently chatting to her in Hungarian and wanted Sarah to play with her and to show her toys to her. It was very funny to watch.

We visited Devon and stayed a few nights at Haze's home as well. We hardly talked about Luke's illness; we tried to be as normal as we could. The daily nausea and vomiting were already normal now and we tried to make it as easy to deal with as possible. God gave me the strength to do everything.

Over the summer we also took a little break at the hospice. Luke enjoyed the music therapy and slept outside in the garden for his afternoon nap. While he was asleep, James and I managed to eat lunch together in the garden without interruption, which meant a lot for us. Another time, we went for a family bike ride using a very clever tricycle from the hospice; it has a child seat on the front, you pedal from the rear, and it also folds into a buggy. We all enjoyed the ride and fell in love immediately with the tricycle, so later that evening we found a second-hand one on eBay to buy for home.

Luke's next scan was in August and when we got the phone call that the result was stable yet again we were delighted. Then, unexpectedly, a few days later we received another phone call. They had found something on the scan pictures after all. One particular person who had seen all Luke's scans from the beginning noticed something that everyone had missed when they looked at the scan pictures the first time, but when it had been pointed out, they all agreed with him. It was a new growth and again in a difficult place. They couldn't operate but would wait and see what the next scan showed and how quickly it changed.

I felt quite down but strived to remain strong. The voice was still there: "Everything is going to be fine."

We had another request for the doctors: I desperately wanted to go to Hungary. While Luke remained relatively stable, they agreed we could go.

We prayed a lot, and asked other people to pray, that we would have a smooth journey as we had decided to go by train over six countries, a journey that took thirty-two hours. We were anxious that Luke wouldn't like the train as he is often scared of unfamiliar and loud noises and environments. We went on a practice trip to Bristol because we hadn't travelled by train since he was a tiny baby. He cried most of the way there. The train back was better though and we had the confidence to go ahead and book the journey. Despite our initial concern, we believed it would be better than flying for a variety of reasons, and hopefully fun. (It was.) James researched and organised the journey really well and we had a fantastic time.

Europe was dealing with lots of migration at this time and many of the regular international train routes were temporarily suspended. Eri Mama came with us; without her, I'm not sure how we would have managed with the ten bags we had to take along. This included an oxygen cylinder bag and a spare second suction machine in case ours broke in any way, plus Luke's clothes and medicines and daily care items. We had already sent a pallet containing nine large boxes with most of his medical supplies, suction catheters, feed, syringes, and our clothes to my parent's house in Hungary where we would be staying for the majority of the time.

Luke was brilliant on the train. He enjoyed it and coped amazingly, including sleeping well on the sleeper train. We set off from Bath to London in the morning, then took the Eurostar to Brussels, followed by a train to Cologne. That evening we caught the sleeper to Vienna and, when we arrived there in the morning, the train to Budapest. It actually went directly to the airport which was handy because that's where we were hiring a car from to drive to my village, a couple of hours' further travelling.

We were so happy to see family and close friends after two years without visiting. The dates of our trip meant we spent our fifth wedding anniversary in my village, the place where we had got married, and we went for a lovely walk by the church and castle. It was a special time. We also celebrated Ocsi Papa's birthday. Because we had lots of visitors each day and only seven days to be together with my family, we decided to have a day trip and drove over to the famous nearby wine town of Tokaj. We ate a tasty sit-down lunch in a restaurant and then walked along the river and through the old town. James tried to buy some wine to take back to the UK but there was too much choice, which caused much stress!

After a week in my village we went to Budapest, where one of my cousins was getting married. It was nice to see everyone again. We had a lovely lunch with some very special friends of the family – Adel, Tibi and Laura. After lunch, Luke had a really good sleep while James and Tibi took our hire car back to the airport.

Leaving Hungary was very sad but on the other hand we were very grateful to God that we had been able to do it at all. Of course, Ocsi Papa and Uncle Bence could still visit us, but it would not be the same as being back in Hungary, at home and seeing lots of people.

We had a good return journey and this time had more sightseeing time in Cologne and Brussels. It was fun to be a tourist for a while!

We arrived back on Monday evening and were pleased to be back safely, without Luke having needed any medical treatment, especially as we hadn't been able to get any travel insurance to cover him. We were 'back to reality' and facing everything that that brings.

Within a few days of our return, Luke became very ill, and it turned out after numerous X-rays, courses of antibiotics and hospital admissions that he had pneumonia. Every single week over the next two months we ended up in hospital. During this period, he had his MRI scan again and the result was stable. We were really glad not to need to worry about multiple things at the same time, so we could concentrate on the pneumonia. Unfortunately, to compound his respiratory problems, he also suffered a collapsed lung as a result of the general anaesthetic but this corrected itself shortly afterwards. Next he had a bad cold, which was actually para-flu. At his lowest point he spent days simply lying on the sofa on oxygen 24/7, and he was on the oxygen saturation monitor with its familiar alarms and constantly changing number display. In addition, he was still vomiting five times a day, something that had been going on for months.

After a couple of weeks, we felt Luke was doing better; he had a little energy back and managed to crawl around the room slowly once again, and he played happily. But suddenly he was much weaker and sleepier every day. He didn't want to play with any of his toys and asked to go to sleep, which was unusual. He had one particular night of crying where nothing would stop him, and we knew it wasn't like him; we knew something was wrong. I was a bit concerned that his shunt had blocked, causing a build-up of pressure in his brain, and it stayed at the back of my mind.

I told James and he called Sarah about our concerns. She said we should go into our local hospital. There the doctor agreed to a CT scan to check his shunt. It turned out I was right – his shunt had blocked – and so we had another blue-light ambulance transfer to Bristol and later that night he had an operation to replace it. Looking back, his crying was just like the crying prior to his tumour being discovered; both were his response to the increased pressure in his brain.

One miraculous thing happened when we took Luke to the anaesthetic room for this operation. James was holding him while I was sitting myself down to take him on to my lap for the anaesthetic fluid to be injected. Just then Luke called out to me, put his hands together and said, "Amen." I asked James if he had noticed what just happened. I wondered how on earth Luke had had time to say this or know what was going to happen with him and ask me to pray for him. I said, "Yes, my darling, I will pray for you, and don't worry. God bless you. We will see you again soon and you will feel better." I wasn't worried. I prayed that night and thanked God for him.

What an amazing, special son! *My* son. God is truly in him. I don't think all children are that gifted to see God's presence. I am truly blessed to witness this with my own eyes.

After the operation Luke felt much better and he was himself again. We celebrated a lovely Christmas and in January received the great news that his latest MRI scan was stable.

We wanted to make life as normal as we could for him, and so in February he started preschool. To think of leaving him in other people's care to manage all his medical and physical needs was scary, but at the same time we knew that it was right to do. We couldn't give him more because he needed specialised teachers around him for his educational development, and we hoped that being with other children more would be good for him.

CHAPTER TEN

Final Thoughts

Anyone who believes in him will not be disappointed. ... Anyone who calls on the name of the Lord will be saved.

Romans 10:11,13

You might ask how I recognise God's presence in Luke. Well, one example is when we are talking about things that we want to do. For instance, James and I had a conversation about our financial giving to church, which happened to be in front of Luke. We made our decision and then Luke grabbed my neck and James' neck, bringing the three of us closely together, and hugged and kissed us: We knew that was from God, that he was showing how he was pleased. It's not just about church; it's about love as well. Luke senses when is the best time to kiss us or hug us.

I won't list everything because on paper it would be too much, but I've described some of the things that I call miracles.

131

I realise that I have a very special son. He has showed me how not to be afraid of anything, particularly his illness, and not to be disappointed. God is in him and doing amazing things through him with me. His spirit is so big, and I have learned that whatever happens to him or to us – even death – everything is going to be OK. God never leaves you. Never!

When you're going through a difficult time, it's natural to ask, "Why is this happening?" God knows the answer and things happen according to his timing. The answer may come to us in this world or maybe in heaven, but you have to trust in him in all situations.

I wasn't a 'big Christian' and I had no idea what it was all about, but I believe that you can find God at any point and in any circumstances during your lifetime, just as I did. It's never too late. God was there, always around me, but I didn't reach out to him. I can identify with Job's story in the Bible. If you don't normally read the Bible, here's a good reason to start! Read the story for yourself in the Book of Job, or online at biblegateway.com. I would recommend skipping the chapters of conversation with his friends because they don't know what they are talking about, but the conversation between Job and God is amazing. Job questions God as to why he has let him get hurt, taking his children away and making him ill.

God has taught me through Luke to fully trust in him even when my prayers don't get answered straightaway or when the miracle isn't evident. He has given me such power to cope with Luke's illness, a true life, freedom from pain, courage to stay in my marriage through the ups and downs; but also he has brought me joy and happiness in the sad times. It is amazing, and I love the Lord for this. Luke's light will always be in my life.

Find your peace in God and remind yourself that you will receive a better life in heaven. Because you will.

I thank God that James is in my life. I have found that marriage can work even in the midst of very challenging circumstances. We still have some difficult days but not with such huge arguments, and we respect each other and help each other with daily life. James is the love of my life and five years' marriage isn't enough – we want to be together forever!

Now at the time of writing, Luke is very much alive and he is with us, providing joy and miracles in our everyday life. However, his doctors have told us he won't have a long life. We are ready for this, even if we don't want to be. There will be an emptiness but we are already full of thanksgiving to God that Luke was born into our lives and that we could be his parents.

One day I had a chat with my friend Mandy and this is how she sees Luke: "I have observed that all children develop at different rates. Whilst one might be quick to crawl, another might learn to talk or build a tower of bricks. Whilst Luke has been unable to develop some skills, he has been developing others. His understanding and awareness seem quite remarkable. His love of music and his connection with worship, music and prayer is very special. He has a quiet patience and yet he can be very clear when someone behaves or speaks inappropriately with him. I love him to bits!"

Yes, he might be behind a little physically, but he understands everything that is happening to him and around him.

Finally, if having read this story you want to invite God into your life too, you can say a simple prayer and from then on just pray daily. Thank him that you can get up in the morning, thank him for your life, and pray that you will be safe because he is with you.

> *Lord Jesus Christ,*
>
> *I am sorry for the things I have done wrong in my life [take a few minutes to ask his forgiveness for anything particular that is on your conscience]. Please forgive me. I now turn from everything that I know is wrong.*
>
> *Thank you that you died on the cross for me so that I could be forgiven and set free.*
>
> *Thank you that you offer me forgiveness and the gift of your Spirit. I now receive that gift.*
>
> *Please come into my life by your Holy Spirit to be with me forever. Thank you, Lord Jesus.*
>
> *Amen.* [29]

---

[29] From 'Why Jesus' by Nicky Gumbel.

Postscript

I always liked poems and I try and think about what the author was feeling when he or she wrote the words down. One of my favourite Hungarian poems is from the late Jozsef Ratkó. This is the first version in English as I asked his wife's permission for it to be translated.

The poem always shows me how mothers cannot be broken and how they cope with everything, just like Mary did in the Bible. It shows how life taught me to be strong in any circumstances and I'm hoping for other mums who are suffering to trust in God and give their hopes to God when they are in the dark. Here is a passage from the poem:

Hymn to My Mother

Mothers are immortal.
They just switch body, face, shape;
Not one of them is dead –
They are as young as time.
Reborn with each new child,
*   they die with each new passing,*
Only to rise at dawn on the third day.
Let them be given beauty,
Eternal devotion for their love,
And let them have tears too,
So they can bear the whole world's pain.

József Ratkó

I have found that music helps as well. When I listen to the following lyrics, God reminds me he is here with me. I love this song and can play it over and over; it gives me strength again and again.

Oceans (Where Feet May Fail) [30]

You call me out upon the waters
The great unknown where feet may fail
And there I find you in the mystery
In oceans deep
My faith will stand

And I will call upon Your name
And keep my eyes above the waves
When oceans rise
My soul will rest in Your embrace
For I am Yours and You are mine

Your grace abounds in deepest waters
Your sovereign hand
Will be my guide
Where feet may fail and fear surrounds me
You've never failed and You won't start now

So I will call upon Your name
And keep my eyes above the waves
When oceans rise
My soul will rest in Your embrace
For I am Yours and You are mine

Spirit lead me where my trust is without borders
Let me walk upon the waters
Wherever You would call me
Take me deeper than my feet could ever wander
And my faith will be made stronger
In the presence of my Saviour

---

[30] Hillsong; used by permission

My Mighty Son

Oh, Jesus, you're my God!

I will call upon Your name
Keep my eyes above the waves
My soul will rest in Your embrace
I am Yours and You are mine

Another favourite song of mine is Laughing With by Regina Spektor. You can find the lyrics at:

www.metrolyrics.com/laughing-with-lyrics-regina-spektor.html

Or just scan the QR-barcode below with your smartphone:

Thank You!

We have been very fortunate to receive assistance (financial, practical or emotional) from the following charities:

- Clic Sargent
- Childrens' Hospice South West
- Ronald McDonald House Bristol
- Promise Dreams
- Family Fund
- Bath Children's Cancer Fund
- React
- Rainbow Trust
- Torbay Holiday Helper's Network

A big thank you to them and their supporters for making it all possible.

Find Out More!

To contact the author or see more photos, check out our website:

www.mymightyson.co.uk

Or simply scan the QR-barcode below with your smartphone:

James, Luke and Virág